Leading Cases in Song

Leading Cases in Song

A Lawyer's Companion

Stephen Todd

Illustrations by Murray Nicol

Musical format arrangement by John Pattinson

PUBLISHED BY:
Brookers Ltd
Level 4, NEC House
40 Taranaki St
Wellington

ISBN: 978-0-86472-844-9

PREFACE

More than 20 years ago students in the Law School at the University of Canterbury in New Zealand decided to put on a Law Revue. The students asked members of staff if they would like to contribute, and I thought of offering a short song about the decision of the House of Lords in *Donoghue v Stevenson*. This first attempt was rather amateurish, but the Revue was a hit and soon became an established part of the academic year at Canterbury.

I made a few more attempts in later years, and eventually, at the suggestion of one of my daughters, I decided to try to write a book of songs, including some short operas, based for the most part on leading or well-known decisions of the courts in the UK and the US. And here is the result. Not all of the cases are of major legal significance, but all are notable at least by reason of their facts or the interesting legal issues that they involve.

My criteria in choosing suitable decisions were two-fold. The positive requirements were that the case should be some or all of entertaining/interesting/odd/bizarre. The negative requirements were that it should not be boring/offensive/tragic, where light verse would not be appropriate. I hope that all of the songs can be seen to fall on the right side of the line in applying these criteria. They all seek to give a light-hearted take on the case concerned.

The songs are all based upon the songs and music of the Gilbert and Sullivan operas. Obviously the words are new, although occasionally words or lines from Sir William Gilbert seemed particularly apt and could be adapted in some suitable way. As regards the music, Sir Arthur Sullivan's work has many virtues, chief of which are that it is memorable, cheerful and great fun. It was ideal for a project of this kind.

It seemed to me that a book of songs about decisions of the courts would be greatly enhanced by including some illustrations. Fortunately I was able to call upon Murray Nicol, a very talented illustrator and cartoonist, to provide them. His drawings exceeded my highest expectations. Readers can judge for themselves in the following pages.

I was also helped a great deal by John Pattinson, who produced the score and made all necessary adaptations of the original music to the songs we have here. The songs work better when they are actually sung, and including the score makes singing them possible or at least a good deal easier.

In the following pages the heading to each song includes the Gilbert and Sullivan opera and song on which it is based. Readers who would like a simple method for listening to the music should go to the Gilbert and Sullivan Archive on the internet, click on the opera concerned, then the web opera, then the song. At the top of each song there is a karaoke icon which will play the tune. It may need adapting in some way to its new application here, and the score provided at the back of the book will show how this has been done.

One pretty obvious point about this book needs to be made. The songs take their inspiration from what happened in the cases concerned, but no more than that. They are not law reports. A degree of (poetic?) licence may have been taken with the particular facts and/or the arguments of counsel and/or the reasoning of the judges. The songs are not intended to say anything about anyone actually involved in the cases. (Even more obviously, nor are the illustrations.) And to the extent that there is a message to be drawn from any particular song, the sentiment in the last verse of the last song applies throughout the book as a whole.

It may be that there are many more cases which would be suitable for turning into songs in the way that has been done here. I would be delighted to receive suggestions from readers. Please feel free to email me at Stephen.Todd@canterbury.ac.nz .

I wish to thank all those persons working for Thomson Reuters in New Zealand who have assisted in bringing this book to publication. I would like to pay particular tribute to Ian McIntosh, the Commercial Manager, for his efforts in turning the idea of publishing a book of songs about court decisions into reality, and to Bridget Giblin, the Managing Editor, for her excellent work in actually producing the book.

There are tentative plans to produce a CD of some of the songs. The publishers will give information about this in due course.

Lawyers and non-lawyers alike enjoy jokes and amusing anecdotes about the legal profession and the law generally. I certainly hope that the readers of this book will find it entertaining. I hope as well that Gilbert and Sullivan fans will like the new treatment of some of their favourite songs.

Stephen Todd

Law School, University of Nottingham

6 November 2013

For Kirsten, Lucy, Alison and Rebecca

STEPHEN TODD

Stephen Todd is a Professor of Law at the University of Canterbury in New Zealand and Professor of Common Law at the University of Nottingham in England. He is particularly interested in the law of torts and the law of contract and has published widely in these fields.

MURRAY NICOL

Murray Nicol did the drawings.

JOHN PATTINSON

John Pattinson is a retired Senior Lecturer from the University of Canterbury and continues to be actively engaged as a conductor, pianist, broadcaster and lecturer. His main field of interest is opera, both as conductor and lecturer.

CONTENTS

OPERA

SONGS

OPERA

SONGS

OPERA

SONGS

APPENDIX

CASES

(In order of citation)

(Cases in bold have their own songs or parts of songs)

***Carlill v Carbolic Smoke Ball Co* [1893] 1 QB 256**

Fisher v Bell [1961] 1 QB 394

Thornton v Shoe Lane Parking Ltd [1971] 2 QB 163

Pharmaceutical Society of Great Britain v Boots Cash Chemists (Southern) Ltd [1952] 2 QB 795

Foakes v Beer (1884) 9 App Cas 605

Shogun Finance Ltd v Hudson [2004] 1 AC 919

Royal Bank of Scotland Plc v Etridge [2002] 2 AC 773

***Leonard v Pepsico Inc* 88 F Supp 2d 116 (1999)**

***Chaplin v Hicks* [1911] 2 KB 786**

***Re Brocklehurst* [1978] 1 All ER 767**

***R v Davie* (1979) 48 CCC (2d) 571**

***Donoghue v Stevenson* [1932] AC 562**

***Tutton v AD Walter Ltd* [1986] QB 61**

***Christy Bros Circus v Turnage* 144 SE 680 (1928)**

***Homer v Long* 599 A 2d 1193 (1992)**

***Corso v Crawford Dog and Cat Hospital* 415 NYS 2d 182 (1979)**

McFarlane v Tayside Health Board [2000] 2 AC 59

Calvert v William Hill Credit Ltd [2009] 2 WLR 1065

Sayers v Harlow UDC [1958] 1 WLR 623

***Zepeda v Zepeda* 190 NE 2d 849 (1963)**

***Pelman v McDonald's Corp* 237 F Supp 2d 512 (SDNY 2003)**

***Burton v Crowell Publishing Co* 82 F 2d 154 (1936)**

***Berkoff v Burchill* [1996] 4 All ER 1008**

Sim v Stretch [1936] 2 All ER 1237

Youssoupoff v Metro-Goldwyn-Mayer (1934) 50 TLR 581

Scott v Sampson (1882) 8 QBD 491

Parmiter v Coupland (1840) 151 ER 340

Allason v BBC Worldwide The Times, 22 January 1998

Radio 2UE Sydney Pty Ltd v Chesterton [2009] HCA 16

Cornwell v Myskow [1987] 1 WLR 630

Liberace v Daily Mirror The Times, 18 June 1959

***Charleston v News Group Newspapers Ltd* [1995] 2 WLR 450**

***Campbell v MGN Ltd* [2004] 2 AC 457**

***Mosley v News Group Newspapers Ltd* [2008] EWHC 1777**

Kaye v Robertson [1991] FSR 62

HRH Prince of Wales v Associated Newspapers Ltd [2008] Ch 57

Douglas v Hello! Ltd [2008] 1 AC 1

Duchess of Argyll v Duke of Argyll [1967] Ch 302

Jagger v Darling [2005] EWHC 683

***R v Brown* [1994] 1 AC 212**

***Ferguson v British Gas Trading Ltd* [2010] 1 WLR 785**

***British Chiropractic Assoc v Singh* [2011] 1 WLR 133**

MRS CARLILL
AND THE
AMAZING CARBOLIC SMOKEBALL

AN OPERA IN TWO ACTS

(Based on *Carlill v Carbolic Smoke Ball Co* [1893] 1 QB 256)

CAST

Lecturers

Mrs Carlill

Smokeball vendor

Clerk of the court

Counsel for Mrs Carlill

Counsel for the Carbolic Smokeball Co

Lord Justice Bowen

Lord Justice Lindley

Lord Justice A L Smith

Chorus

ACT I

Our Question for the Day Asks if a Promise is Contractual

(Music: THE PIRATES OF PENZANCE: "I Am the Very Model of a Modern Major General")

Lecturers

Our question for the day asks if a promise is contractual

We wonder if it's animal or vegetable or mineral

A makes a deal with party B, and C when it's collateral

With words or – sometimes – acts that aren't in any way equivocal

We search the books to find out all the principles historical

There's *Fisher*, where the flick-knife on display was invitational[1]

Or *Thornton*, where the parking ticket's terms were mechanistical[2]

And Messrs Boots the chemist with their matters pharmaceutical[3]

Chorus

And Messrs Boots the chemist with their matters pharmaceutical

And Messrs Boots the chemist with their matters pharmaceutical

And Messrs Boots the chemist with their matters pharmaceuti-ceuti-cal

Lecturers

We need consideration for the making of a promise or

A promisee cannot enforce a bargain with a promisor

---

1   *Fisher v Bell* [1961] 1 QB 394.
2   *Thornton v Shoe Lane Parking Ltd* [1971] 2 QB 163.
3   *Pharmaceutical Society of Great Britain v Boots Cash Chemists (Southern) Ltd* [1952] 2 QB 795.

So where a debt is paid in part the rule applies in *Foakes and Beer*

But estoppel undercuts the rule and paints on top a fresh veneer

Suppose that now a villain says he's A when he is really B

Then *Shogun* will avoid the deal in matters of identity

And what about a contract truly made between just A and B

But C then wants to claim a share and beat the rule of privity?

Chorus

But C then wants to claim a share and beat the rule of privity?

But C then wants to claim a share and beat the rule of privity?

But C then wants to claim a share and beat the rule of privi-privi-ty?

(Lecturer 1 is getting increasingly excited as he expounds upon the core principles of the law of contract)

Lecturers

A promise cannot operate with horrid illegality

A bargain falls beside the way if one lacks full capacity

But where there is a contract that is broken fundamentally

Which has a term excluding this, there's no responsibility

Our next concern's a party who contracts uncon-scion-ab-a-ly

Here *Etridge* serves to save the day, invoking rules of equity[5]

And also where a contract's made in terms that lack morality

Lord Denning comes to take a stand and judge all claims right-mindedly

Chorus

Lord Denning comes to take a stand and judge all claims right-mindedly

Lord Denning comes to take a stand and judge all claims right-mindedly

Lord Denning comes to take a stand and judge all claims right-minded-minded-ly

*(Enter two men in white coats, who drag off lecturer 1 in a highly emotional state.
Lecturers 2 and 3 continue)*

....

3   *Foakes v Beer* (1884) 9 App Cas 605.
4   *Shogun Finance Ltd v Hudson* [2004] 1 AC 919.
5   *Royal Bank of Scotland Plc v Etridge* [2002] 2 AC 773.

Lecturers 2 and 3

So whether it is animal or vegetable or mineral
We now know what it takes to find a promise that's contractual
All's well where happily 'tis clear that everything's consensual
Yet breaking deals without a care becomes most disputational
And turning now to *Carlill* and the claim 'bout fumes carbolical
The question's if the smokeball pledge is legally enforceable
A contract with the world at large is surely inconceivable
But don't forget that deals are made when contract's unilateral

Chorus

But don't forget that deals are made when contract's unilateral
But don't forget that deals are made when contract's unilateral
But don't forget that deals are made when contract's uni-uni-lateral

All

And turning now to *Carlill* and the claim 'bout fumes carbolical
The question's if the smokeball pledge is legally enforceable
A contract with the world at large is surely inconceivable
But don't forget that deals are made when contract's unilateral

(Chorus moves to side of stage, lecturers leave)

Behold the Smokeball Flu Preventioner

(Music: THE MIKADO: "Behold the Lord High Executioner")

(Smokeball vendor at stall, with smokeball contraption displayed at front and poster prominently advertising his wares)

Smokeball vendor

Behold the smokeball flu preventioner

A remedy that's surely efficacious

No aches or chills or influenza nor

All other ills or ailments or distempers

(Enter Mrs Carlill)

Chorus

Inhale, inhale

With the smokeball flu preventioner

Inhale, inhale

With the wonder ball, with the wonder ball

With the smokeball flu pre-ven-tion-er

Smokeball vendor

A reward that's found with every ball

A guarantee that's safe and satisfact'ry

One hundred pounds, we'll gladly pay to all

Who sniff the ball yet still become unhealthy

(Mrs Carlill is impressed. Vendor demonstrates using the ball)

Chorus

Inhale, inhale

With the smokeball flu preventioner

Inhale, inhale

With the wonder ball, with the wonder ball
With the smokeball flu pre-ven-tion-er

Mrs Carlill

Here's a very curious tale
No need then to take one's chances
Surely found the Holy Grail
With some guaranteed finances
For you simply must inhale
Then your health the ball enhances
And if then they make a sale
Under such like circumstances
Sadly should their cure-all fail
Due to sorrowful mischances
"Alas, I'm ill" you wail
"Yet they've good recognizances"

Mrs Carlill

Here's a very curious tale
No need then to take one's chances
Surely found the Holy Grail
For you simply must inhale

Chorus

Here's a very curious tale
No need then to take one's chances
Surely found the Holy Grail
For you simply must inhale

All

Inhale, inhale
With the smokeball flu preventioner
Inhale, inhale
With the wonder ball, with the wonder ball
With the smokeball flu pre-ven-tion-er

(Mrs Carlill takes a smokeball, puts head over contraption for holding it. Loud gasps, gurgles and sniffs. Lights fade)

(Spotlight on Mrs Carlill as she slowly enters the stage, looking pale and woebegone)

Poor Suffering Me

(Music: THE PIRATES OF PENZANCE: "Poor Wandering One")

Mrs Carlill

Poor suff'ring me
I'm feeble, I'm sickly, I'm wretched
Breathed in the steam
Living a dream
Poor suffering me
Poor suff'ring me
I'm ailing, I'm catching a chill
Swallowed their tales
The remedy fails
I'm poorly, I'm suff'ring, I'm ill

Chorus

Take heart, don't worry, don't pine
Fight, sue, the money, it's thine

Mrs Carlill

Take heart, fair days will shine
I'll sue then, the money, it's mine

Chorus

Take heart, don't worry, don't pine
Sue for the money, it's certainly thine

Mrs Carlill

Take heart fair days will shine
I'll sue then, the money, it's mine
Ah! Ah! Ah! Ah!
Poor suff'ring me

I'm feeble, I'm sickly, I'm wretched
I'll mop and I'll mope
But still there is hope
Of wealth for poor suffering me
Ah! Ah! Ah! Ah! Ah! Ah! Ah! Ah! Ah! Ah! Ah! Ah!
Fair days will shine
Ah! Ah! Ah! Ah! Ah! Ah! (x32)
Fair days will shine
Ah! Ah! Ah! Ah! Ah! Ah! (x32)

Chorus

Take heart, don't worry, don't pine
Sue for the money, it's thine

Mrs Carlill

Ah! Ah! Ah! Ah!
It's mine

(Blackout)

ACT 2

(Courtroom scene. Judges on the bench, counsel at tables on either side)

Silence in Court

(Music: TRIAL BY JURY: "All Hail Great Judge")

Clerk of the court

Silence in court

Silence in court

And all attention lend

Behold your judges

In due submission bend

My Lords, We Make a Claim Today

(Music: TRIAL BY JURY: "When I Good Friends Was Called to the Bar")

Counsel for Mrs Carlill

My Lords, we make a claim today
'Bout the making of a bargain
The plaintiff read and did obey
A poster's specious jargon
She used the ball but caught the flu
And met the stipulation
And from this court she claims her due
In merited compensation

Chorus

And from this court she claims her due
In merited compensation

Counsel for Mrs Carlill

The comp'ny says they need not pay
Claims nothing said was binding
But a deal's a deal, and of this they may
Need constantly reminding
Used twists and turns, they've ducked and dived
And given no slightest quarter
But judgment day has now arrived
And pay we say they oughter

Chorus

But judgment day has now arrived
And pay we say they oughter

Counsel for the Carbolic Smoke Ball Company

The plaintiff's flu we do concede
Her aches and pains and sickness
But for riches now she's come to plead
With unbecoming quickness
The plaintiff's nasty cold and cough
Is one of life's mischances
But she's aimed her snout right at the trough
In the hope of cash advances

Chorus

But she's aimed her snout right at the trough
In the hope of cash advances

Counsel for the Carbolic Smoke Ball Company

The poster's words were but a puff
A bet or gaming wager
Consideration not enough
'Twas an act of God, vis major
To your Lordships learn'd in common law
We extend our invitation
Throw out this suit, this claim of straw
With clear disapprobation

Chorus

To your Lordships learn'd in common law
We extend our invitation
Throw out this suit, this claim of straw
With clear disapprobation

(Judges go into huddle)

The Gazette of Pall Mall

(Music: THE MIKADO: "The Criminal Cried")

Judges

The Gazette of Pall Mall did announce to us all
'Bout a cure that quite wonderfully
Will stop the flu if you buy the ball
And sniff it assiduously
The company said that money was paid
With a trusty depositee
A reward to all those who used their nose
To show its sincerity
Sincerity

Oh never shall we
Quite thoughtlessly
Forget that depositee
When taking our view
About all that is due
From this claim of sincerity

Chorus

We know them well
They always tell
A false or groundless tale
They usually try
To utter a lie
And rarely do they fail

Lord Justice Bowen

A wondrous ball mused Mrs Carlill
From flu she'd always be free

She'd never, she thought, be poorly or ill
So grabbed one immediately
Her head soon enwreathed, she giddily breathed
As under a sheet dove she
She sniffled and snuffled and gurgled and guggled
As she breathed in that pot-pourri
That pot-pourri

Judges

Oh never shall we
Forget that she
Inhaled very earnestly
As we ponder anew
'Bout everything due
When she breathed in that pot-pourri

Chorus

Most clearly she
Impassionedly
Sniffed optimistically
Not even a sneeze
A cough or a wheeze
From breathing carbolically

Lord Justice Lindley

The plaintiff performed her side of the pact
Not telling defendant (D)
Yet taking D's word and doing an act
Is perfectly good for me
When calamity came and sick she became
To the comp'ny she entered a plea
Saying "Now that I've done it please pay for I've won it"
And she claimed on the guarantee
The guarantee

Judges

Oh never shall we
Forget her plea
Or the sniffle that sniffl-ed she
She still caught the flu
Sought money in lieu
By her claim on the guarantee

Chorus

It's clear her act
Performed the pact
Albeit not known to D
When calamity came
And sick she became
She'd acted reliantly

Lord Justice A L Smith

The claim was denied "It's not fair" it was cried
"There's no liability
'Twas a wager or bet, its terms far too wide
'Twill last for eternity"
Yet the plaintiff relied on words that implied
A no-frills expectancy
Not simply a puff, the words were enough
To be taken most seriously
Most seriously

Judges

Oh never shall we
Forget that she
Did sniff most expectantly
Not simply a puff
The words were enough
To be taken most seriously

Chorus

This terrible tale
You can't assail
With truth it quite agrees
For faultless fact
Her claim exact
Which now they must appease

Judges

So take every care with your garlanded tales
'Bout the wonders your nostrum will do
For if after all it unhappily fails
Then so much the worse for you
If you brag and you huff with silver-tongued puff
Your goods and your chattels to boost
On making a deal you pay for your zeal
And your chickens come home to roost
Come home to roost

So never should you
Not think things through
With quackery chattels to boost
On making a deal
You pay for your zeal
And your chickens come home to roost

All

So never should you
Not think things through
With quackery chattels to boost
On making a deal
You pay for your zeal
And your chickens come home to roost

Come home, come home, come home
Come home to roost

FINIS

Pepsi-points

(Based on *Leonard v Pepsico Inc* 88 F Supp 2d 116 (1999), aff'd 210 F 3d 88 (2000))
(Music: TRIAL BY JURY: "When First My Old, Old Love I Knew")

Narrator

Now let's salute stout Mrs Carlill

No doubt the reader recalls

She sadly caught a cold and chill

After sniffing those balls

She made a deal and got the loot

The comp'ny had promised to pay

Now here's another likely suit

In far off USA

Far off U, far off U, far off U

Chorus

USA

Narrator

Far off U, far off U, far off U

Chorus

USA

Narrator and Chorus

Now here's another likely suit

In far off USA

Narrator

Our story begins with Pepsico

Anxious 'bout making a profit

Keen to market their drink, and so

People buy lot and lots of it

On sales of the fizz, by a "pepsi-point" scheme
In a plan most cunning and shrewd
Buyers all given a right to redeem
For widgets, with points they'd accrued
Very shrewd, very shrewd, very shrewd

Chorus

Cunning plan

Narrator

Very shrewd, very shrewd, very shrewd

Chorus

Cunning plan

Narrator and Chorus

Buyers all given a right to redeem
For widgets, with points they'd accrued

Narrator

An ad on TV one summery day
In terms not very Socratic
Told all about this scheme in a way
That might be called melodramatic
Boys sample Pepsi with gusto and glee
While points for the goods flash before us
When all of a sudden the good that we see
Becomes extra loud and enormous
'Normous size, 'normous size, 'normous size

Chorus

Special prize

Narrator

'Normous size, 'normous size, 'normous size

Chorus

Special prize

Narrator and Chorus

When all of a sudden the good that we see
Becomes extra loud and enormous

Narrator

Hurricane winds now enter the tale
With booms and crashes and thunder
A teacher is stripped by the storm and the gale
Leaving his wear that was under
Then all is revealed and we see the new prize
And what we are going to get
For landing in front of our goggling eyes
A Harrier AV 8 jet[1]
V 8 jet, V 8 jet, V 8 jet

Chorus

Jumping jet

Narrator

V 8 jet, V 8 jet, V 8 jet

Chorus

Jumping jet

Narrator and Chorus

For landing in front of our goggling eyes
A Harrier AV 8 jet

1   The advertisement can be viewed at www.youtube.com/watch?v=ZdackF2H7Qc.

Narrator

Our plaintiff, John Leonard, had jets on the brain
As a tot at the table he'd thump
And shout "I want a military plane
Especially one that will jump"
So wondered at once about what he had seen
And how many points he would need
The answer he found at the base of the screen
Seven million points was decreed
Seven mill, seven mill, seven mill

Chorus

Million points

Narrator

Seven mill, seven mill, seven mill

Chorus

Million points

Narrator and Chorus

The answer he found at the base of the screen

Seven million points there decreed

Narrator

"I wonder just how many points that I've got"

Mused our hero, his hopes very high

On checking it seemed that it wasn't a lot

Fifteen! he found with a sigh

That left him with too much to drink, and hence

He turned to the rules where he saw

That a point could be bought at a cost of ten cents

So he bought seven million more[2]

Seven mill, seven mill, seven mill

Chorus

Million more

Narrator

Seven mill, seven mill, seven mill

Chorus

Million more

Narrator and Chorus

A point could be bought at a cost of ten cents

So he bought seven million more

Narrator

Fired off a letter to Pepsico

Claiming his Harrier jet

A cheque for the points as the quid pro quo

....

2   More accurately, 6,999, 985.

All the conditions now met
Awaiting, impatient, his promised reward
He found with increasing chagrin
He waited in vain, his letter ignored
For sadly no jump-jet dropped in
All in vain, all in vain, all in vain

Chorus

Nothing came

Narrator

All in vain, all in vain, all in vain

Chorus

Nothing came

Narrator and Chorus

He waited in vain, his letter ignored
Sadly no jump-jet dropped in

Narrator

Our unhappy claimant, with forceful appeal
Went straight way to the court
"It's fraud" he said "They're in breach of the deal
I want the jet that I bought
The commercial misled, the advert deceived
Their practice in trade was unfair
I've reason sufficient to feel a bit peeved
Not getting my military ware"
Feeling peeved, feeling peeved, feeling peeved

Chorus

So deceived

Narrator

Feeling peeved, feeling peeved, feeling peeved

Chorus

So deceived

Narrator and Chorus

Had reason sufficient to feel a bit peeved
Not getting that military ware

Narrator

The rest of this tale I'll sadly relate
A most disappointing report
The claim quickly met an unfortunate fate
Summarily thrown out of court
"'Twas a vision, a simply fantastic jest
In mind of all reasonable folk"
Said the judge, undoubtedly unimpressed
"Nothing more than a joke"
Just a joke, just a joke, just a joke

Chorus

Case dismissed

Narrator

Just a joke, just a joke, just a joke

Chorus

Case dismissed

Narrator and Chorus

The judge undoubtedly unimpressed

Nothing more than a joke

Narrator

So good Mrs C most famously won

Unlucky John Leonard did not

The ad was in fun, JL was undone

This severed the Gordian knot

He was not, it seems, a reasonable man

That person who's oozing with unction

Yet amused us a lot with his pleasing plan

A very commendable function

Pleasing plan, pleasing plan, pleasing plan

Chorus

'Mused us all

Narrator

Pleasing plan, pleasing plan, pleasing plan

Chorus

'Mused us all

Narrator and Chorus

Amused us a lot with his pleasing plan

Very commendable function

An Artful Scheme

(Based on *Chaplin v Hicks* [1911] 2 KB 786)
(Music: THE SORCERER: "Time Was When Love and I Were Well Acquainted")

Narrator

Good Mr Hicks devised a competition

Revealing to us all an artful scheme

For ladies fair, with fame their clear ambition

Aimed at all those who wished to live their dream

Their photographs would demonstrate their beauty

Then readers of a paper had to choose

Fulfilling each their stern, unyielding duty

Chorus

No fear, no fear

Narrator

Selecting who should win and who should lose

Narrator

Miss Chaplin quickly sent an application

And readers soon were able to begin

On exercising keen discrimination

And specifying who they thought should win

All photographs requiring close perusing

'Fore marking who deserved to get their tick

No pondering on who they should be choosing

Chorus

So clear, so clear

Narrator

Decided that Miss Chaplin was their pick

Narrator

Defendant Mr Hicks had further choosing
Selecting from the winners of each heat
But failed this task, his duty thus abusing
So Miss C then unable to compete
Claimed damages on ground of his contracting
To give her an occasion for success
With hope that she would prosper in extracting

Chorus

With hope, with hope

Narrator

Some timely and most generous redress

Narrator

The judges could not come to a decision
Decided (and with each a shifty smile)
That now to test the claim with due precision
Each contestant would clearly need a trial
So all the ladies asked to start parading

And soon 'twas clear the job was fully done
The consequence of all their careful grading?

Chorus

Most fair? Most fair?

Narrator

Determined that Miss Chaplin would have won

Narrator

Now sheepishly I make a full confession
Contritely I must surely bare my soul
For all I've said may cause a misimpression
Telling a story was my only goal
In fact my words are just a little phoney
I'll go further and admit they're quite untrue
And resolutely say they're pure baloney

Narrator and Chorus

Ah me, ah me

Narrator

My aim was simply of diverting you

Narrator

I now will give a proper explanation
And will show why there is nothing untoward
In holding still there should be compensation
Giving Miss C a somewhat large award
For H must pay for contract-breaking action
And certainly we should not look askance
At finding here a right to satisfaction

Chorus

So wise, so wise

Narrator

Although it's clear C only had a chance

Narrator and Chorus

And so her claiming deserved rewarding

Although it's clear her only loss was but a chance

The Baronet and the Garage Man

(Based on *Re Brocklehurst* [1978] 1 All ER 767)
(Music: HMS PINAFORE: "Never mind the why and wherefore")

Judges

Never mind the why and wherefore
Let's forget all ranks, and therefore
Though Sir Philip's station's mighty
Though stupendous be his caste
And his tastes are fine and flighty
He's a noble unsurpassed
Yet here's a gift without regret
Of shooting rights, a well laid plan
Between the friendly baronet
And the lowly garage man

Chorus

Here's a humble garage owner
And aristocratic donor
The Lord of Swy'mley Manor
And eccentric alienor

All

Never mind a person's station
Honest pleb or upper crust
Eat the cake with celebration
Classless be we surely must

Judges

Never mind the why and wherefore

45

Let's forget all ranks, and therefore
We admit the jurisdiction
To pronounce upon the pact
Though may seem a contradiction
Where there's such a classless act
Did influential words and action
Browbeat poor Sir Philip B?
Or did he act without distraction?
Mind at rest, his will quite free?

Chorus

Here's a humble garage owner
And aristocratic donor
The Lord of Swy'mley Manor
And eccentric alienor

All

Never mind a person's station
Honest pleb or upper crust
Eat the cake with celebration
Classless be we surely must

Judges

Never mind the why and wherefore
Let's forget all ranks, and therefore
Though the car man's kin are lowly
And his family cannot pass
He's a person who is wholly
In the lower middle class
Yet Sir Phil can gift the shooting
To one whose blood is hardly blue
– A former junior naval rating –
If he truly wishes to

Chorus

Here's a humble garage owner
And aristocratic donor
The Lord of Swy'mley Manor
And eccentric alienor

All

Never mind a person's station
Honest pleb or upper crust
Eat the cake with celebration
Classless be we surely must

Judges

Never mind the why and wherefore
Let's forget all ranks, and therefore
Here's a gentleman patrician
Who just wanted to enjoy
Friendship with a humble huntsman

Though most surely hoi polloi
Awed by those of noble breeding
Always did what he was told
Sir Phil did all the dominating
Now the garage man's struck gold

Chorus

Here's a humble garage owner
And aristocratic donor
The Lord of Swy'mley Manor
And eccentric alienor

All

Never mind a person's station
Honest pleb or upper crust
Eat the cake with celebration
Classless be we surely must

Is God a Person?

(Based on *R v Davie* (1979) 48 CCC (2d) 571)
(Music*:* IOLANTHE: "The Law is the True Embodiment")

Judge Lander

Defendant (D), unhappily

Is charged with criminality

The crime it's said he did commit?

(Which D does not at all admit)

'Twas starting lots of forest fires

Such conduct clearly ultra vires

Locked up in gaol, and there, unknown

A camera and a microphone

Recorded D, with arms up high

Appeal to God with fervent cry

Chorus

Recorded D, with arms up high

Appeal to God with fervent cry

Judge Lander

"Oh Lord" he prayed "Please give a hand

And let me know your least command

I'll do my penance, say my prayers

Attend my spiritual affairs

But in return please help a bit

Just let me get away with it

Please intervene this once for me

I'll give my thanks eternally

'Twill show your mettle pleasingly

Your transcendental equity"

Chorus

'Twill show your mettle pleasingly
Your transcendental equity

Judge Lander

Confessed his guilt the police now say
But here some law gets in the way
A record made 'lectronic'ly
Needs speaker's sure authority
Or taping's not permissible
The record inadmissible
"But no" says counsel "incorrect
That argument you must reject
The rule most clearly can't apply
To words directed up on high"

Chorus

The rule most clearly can't apply
To words directed up on high

Judge Lander

Now counsel says there needs to be
Communication, definitely
Words must be spoken you to me
By person A to person B
And here, he says, that's not the case
For no such colloquy took place
But can this other person be
Almighty God, the Deity?
The question's rather tricky for
A court applying earthly law

Chorus

The question's rather tricky for
A court applying earthly law

Judge Lander

My mind's made up, I won't convict

The purpose of the law's quite strict
It aims to safeguard talk and chat
That's private – nothing more than that
Here D intended on his own
To speak with God and God alone
At least in law, and legally
God's got some personality
God *is* a person, not a doubt
Although He's everywhere about

Chorus

God *is* a person, not a doubt
Although He's everywhere about

Donoghue v Stevenson

An Opera in Two Acts

(Based on *Donoghue v Stevenson* [1932] AC 562)

CAST
Friend

Mrs Donoghue

Mr Minchella

Mr Stevenson

Lord Atkin

Counsel for Mrs Donoghue

Counsel for Mr Stevenson

Members of the House of Lords

Clerk of the court

Chorus

ACT 1

WELLMEADOW CAFÉ

(Everyone on stage and singing)

We Love the Judges' Law

(Music: HMS PINAFORE: "We Sail the Ocean Blue")

All

We just love the judges' law

Crime, contract, land, and equity

And tort – just give us more

And justice and morality

But the rule we adore o'er the whole of the law

Is the rule of liability

For not taking care with one's head in the air

Unrea-sonab-alee

'ablee, 'ablee, unreasonabalee

'ablee, 'ablee, unreasonabalee

It's the rule we adore we adore all day

We just love the judges' law

Crime, contract, land, and equity

And tort – just give us more

And justice and morality

A rule of liability

For negligent activity

And who will win? – see *Donoghue and Stevenson*

(All leave the stage)

Let's Go To Wellmeadow Café

(Music: HMS PINAFORE: "Little Buttercup")
(Back curtains open to café scene. Enter Mrs Donoghue and friend)

Friend

Hello Mrs Donoghue, sweet Mrs Donoghue

Delighted to meet you today

Let's go for a treat, let's drink and let's eat

Let's go to Wellmeadow Café

Mrs Donoghue

Why certainly yes my dear, that is a good idea

I'm hungry, I'm thirsty, let's fly

An ice cream dessert or a bun or a tart,

And watch the world passing us by

Minchella

Good ladies, kind greeting, delight in your eating

At Paisley's most fabled café

These pastries we're making, the cakes that we're baking

Please choose from our finest array

We've shortbread and toffee, we've tea and we've coffee

Ice cream and some gingery beer

Friend

That sounds just delicious, please hurry and bring us

Two extra-large helpings just here

(Mrs D drinks her ginger beer)

Mrs Donoghue	A glassful to savour – but what a strange flavour
	Odd lumps in my gingery beer
Friend	Oh, tell me just how you are, you've gone all peculiar
	You're looking decidedly queer
Mrs Donoghue	My belly is aching, my insides are quaking
	A decomposed snail in my ale
	I'm feeling all funny, my bowel's gone all runny
	Rush quick and please fetch me a pail

(Friend rushes off stage, returns with bucket,
Mrs D is dramatically sick)

ACT 2

THE HOUSE OF LORDS

(Courtroom scene. Judges' bench at centre stage. Counsel, Mrs Donoghue and friend at table on one side, counsel and Stevenson at table on other.)

Entrance of the Peers

(Music: IOLANTHE: "March of the Peers – trumpet entrance")

(Members of the House of Lords process to the stage from the back of the auditorium and take their places on the bench)

Counsel	Bow, bow, law students in your classes
	Bow, bow, ye lawyers, bow ye masses
	Blow the trumpets, bang the brasses
	Tantantara! Tzing boom!
	Bow, bow, law students in your classes
	Bow, bow, ye lawyers, bow ye masses
	Blow the trumpets, bang the brasses
	Tantantara! Tzing boom!
	(Counsel and their Lordships bow to each other)
Lord Atkin	Esteemed counsel, good morning
Counsel	Sir, good morning
Lord Atkin	I hope you're all quite well

Counsel	Quite well: and you sir?
Lord Atkin	I am in reasonable health, and happy To meet you all once more
Counsel	You do us proud sir

We Are the Judges of the Court of Law

(Music: HMS PINAFORE: "I am the Captain of the Pinafore")

Judges   We are the judges of the court of law

Counsel   And judges of a very good sort

Judges   You're very very good

And be it understood

We're judges of a very good court

Counsel   We're very very good

And be it understood

They're judges of a very good court

Judges   Though we're intellectuelle

We can sing and dance as well

And caper a jig or four

And we're never known to cower

At the words of any lawyer

And we're never, never wrong at law

Counsel   What, never?

Judges   No, never

Counsel   What, never?

Judges	Well, hardly ever
Counsel	They're hardly ever wrong at law
	Then give three cheers and one cheer more
	For the brainy judges of the court of law
	Then give three cheers and one cheer more
	For the judges of the court of law
Judges	We do our best to satisfy you all
Counsel	And with you we're really quite content
Judges	You're exceedingly polite
	And we think it only right
	To return the compliment
Counsel	We're exceedingly polite
	And they think it only right
	To return the compliment
Judges	Bad language or abuse
	We never, never use
	Even faced with a cross QC

Though "bother it" we may
Occasionally say
We never use an F or B

Counsel   What, never?

Judges   No, never

Counsel   What, never?

Judges   Well, hardly ever

Counsel   Hardly ever swear an F or B

Then give three cheers and one cheer more
For the well-bred judges of the court of law
Then give three cheers and one cheer more
For the judges of the court of law

Counsel for Mrs D   My Lords, I call Mrs Donoghue
To tell her tragic tale

Lord Atkin

(Music: THE MIKADO: "Willow, Tit-Willow")

Mrs Donoghue	One day in the summer, a marvellous treat
Chorus	Lord Atkin, Lord Atkin, Lord Atkin
Mrs Donoghue	In Wellmeadow Café, my friend there to meet
Chorus	Lord Atkin, Lord Atkin, Lord Atkin
Mrs Donoghue	An order was made for the best ginger ale
	But added, unknown, was a well brewed-up snail
	I swallowed it down but then let out a wail
Chorus	Lord Atkin, Lord Atkin, Lord Atkin

♪

Mrs Donoghue	I clutched at my belly and fell to the floor
Chorus	Lord Atkin, Lord Atkin, Lord Atkin
Mrs Donoghue	I sicked and I sicked and I sicked up some more
Chorus	Lord Atkin, Lord Atkin, Lord Atkin
Mrs Donoghue	I gasped and I screamed and I sobbed and I sighed
	I howled and I yelled and I moaned and I cried
	An over-cooked gastropod in my inside
Chorus	Lord Atkin, Lord Atkin, Lord Atkin

♪

64

Counsel for S	The claimant, she's faking, no snail in the beer
Chorus	Lord Atkin, Lord Atkin, Lord Atkin
Counsel for S	The fizz in her glass was transparently clear
Chorus	Lord Atkin, Lord Atkin, Lord Atkin
Counsel for S	This court we submit should reject what she's said
	A decomposed snail only there in her head
	A flea in her ear's what she merits instead
Chorus	Lord Atkin, Lord Atkin, Lord Atkin

♪

Counsel for S	Now even accepting her story is true
Chorus	Lord Atkin, Lord Atkin, Lord Atkin
Counsel for S	The mollusc just added some strength to the brew
Chorus	Lord Atkin, Lord Atkin, Lord Atkin
Counsel for S	A claim 'gainst poor S a court cannot invent
	Outrageous a duty would be in extent
	No contract, no payment – there's no precedent
Chorus	Lord Atkin, Lord Atkin, Lord Atkin

♪

65

Counsel for Mrs D	This action concerns an emetic affair
Chorus	Lord Atkin, Lord Atkin, Lord Atkin
Counsel for Mrs D	Where S pertinaciously failed to take care
Chorus	Lord Atkin, Lord Atkin, Lord Atkin
Counsel for Mrs D	See counsel for S as he turns and he twists
	There must be a contract to sue, he insists
	But a claim lies in tort where no contract exists
Chorus	Lord Atkin, Lord Atkin, Lord Atkin

♪

Counsel for Mrs D	The plaintiff we say should most surely succeed
Chorus	Lord Atkin, Lord Atkin, Lord Atkin
Counsel for Mrs D	Ingesting a snail merits payment indeed
Chorus	Lord Atkin, Lord Atkin, Lord Atkin
Counsel for Mrs D	A calamity suffered, we've come to this court
	The maker he did it and pay up he ought
	That snail in the beer is an actionable tort
Chorus	Lord Atkin, Lord Atkin, Lord Atkin
	(General hubbub)

♪

Clerk of the Court	Pray silence in court
	Their Lordships will give their judgment

66

A Rule of Liabilitee

(Music: HMS PINAFORE: "I Am the Ruler of the Queen's Navee")

Judges	We're a court of law and we feel quite free
	To judge this case of great catastrophee
	May Donoghue has had her fill
	Of snails that make her very sadly ill
Chorus	Of snails that make her very sadly ill
Judges	There should we do think most fairly be
	A rule of li-i-a-abilitee
Chorus	There should they do think most fairly be
	A rule of li-i-a-abilitee

♪

Lord Atkin	We hold the manufacturer
	Must pay for snails mixed in the beer
	He must endeavour to ensure
	That slugs don't make his drinks impure
Chorus	That slugs don't make his drinks impure
Lord Atkin	He must surely act more carefullee
	And pay for doing wrong to poorly Mrs D
Chorus	He must surely act more carefullee
	And pay for doing wrong to poorly Mrs D

♪

Lord Atkin	So the maker of the ginger ale
	Is blameful for this sorry tale

His noxious drink, his juice, his brew
Malodorously poisoned Mrs Donoghue

Chorus   Malodorously poisoned Mrs Donoghue

Lord Atkin   He foots the bill and pays the fee
And compensates for failing to be neighbourlee

Chorus   He foots the bill and pays the fee
And compensates for failing to be neighbourlee

♪

Judges   S let the snail crawl in the beer
So for him we say the buck stops here
His fault is clear, he gets the blame
And Mrs Donoghue finds cash and fame

Chorus   And Mrs Donoghue finds cash and fame

Judges and Chorus   She takes her place in historee
And stakes her claim to immortalitee
She takes her place in historee
And stakes her claim to immortalitee

FINIS

Trespassing Bees

(Based on *Tutton v AD Walter Ltd* [1986] QB 61)
(Music: IOLANTHE: "When All Night Long a Chap Remains")

Narrator

We know the fields of England green
Are loved by those who write poetically
But now a plant of alien gene
Intrudes, we think unsympathetically
In art we find from times bygone
The tranquil kine all grazing mellowly
But now we find when gazing on
The fields, we see them shimm'ring yellowly
For threatening this sylvan bower
And something I must now advise
A Herculean fiscal power
The EU now does subsidise
Horizons full of rapeseed flower
By payments of substantial size

Chorus

'Stantial size, 'stantial size
Horizons full of rapeseed flower
And payments of substantial size

Narrator

Here's grower (D) with rare content
His rapeseed growing most sebaceously
But shock! Dismay! With sore torment
Found bugs all chewing quite voraciously
Straightway determined, no debate
And, true to say, with equanimity

These bugs he should exterminate
(Forgetting things in close proximity)
So D began to squirt and spray
A powerful insecticide
The bugs were poisoned right away
No place for nasty pests to hide
But 'twas not all, it's sad to say
Some other little creatures died

Chorus

Creatures died, creatures died
The bugs were poisoned right away
But other little creatures died

Narrator

Let's turn our thoughts to neighbour (P)
A man who's working in his apiary
He's studying the honey bee
And keeping bees (a trifle gingerly)
Observe the bees returning home
A multitude that swarms with noisy buzz
Brings nectar for the honeycomb
For this is what a bee quite often does
P's disposition now irate
His temperament no more at ease
No calm, collected mental state
D's conduct certain to displease
Unhappily, at rapid rate
The grower's spraying killed the bees

Chorus

Killed the bees, killed the bees
Unhappily, at rapid rate
The grower's spraying killed the bees

Narrator

P's claim in law was swift and strong
"D should have sprayed a lot more cautiously

The pois'ning was a civil wrong
Behaved without a doubt most tortiously"
"But no", says D, "hear what I say
The scope of tort's not all-encompassing
Not liable, I need not pay
'Twas very clear the bees were trespassing
As well, take one of rapeseed's traits
Shows why there was no call for care
A scientific view dictates
The bees need not have been just there
The rapeseed flower self-pollinates
So blaming me would not be fair"

71

Chorus

Not be fair, not be fair
The rapeseed flower self-pollinates
So blaming D would not be fair

Narrator

The judge rejected D's reply
"He'd not, D said, at all permitted 'em
Where'er the bees might choose to fly
Would not if asked have then admitted 'em
Yet sure it was those buzzing bees
The rapeseed flowers would seek out tirelessly
My view with *Donoghue* agrees
And D's in breach for acting carelessly"
So thoughtless owners all take heed
Self-interest matters not a jot
When spraying plants you must indeed
– Self-pollinating flowers or not –
Take due account of neighbours' need
Else pay what may be quite a lot

Chorus

Quite a lot, quite a lot
Take due account of neighbours' need
Else pay what may be quite a lot

All of Human Action

(Based on *Christy Bros Circus v Turnage* 144 SE 680 (1928), *Homer v Long* 599 A 2d 1193
(1992) and *Corso v Crawford Dog and Cat Hospital* 415 NYS 2d 182 (1979))
(Music: THE PIRATES OF PENZANCE: "When Frederic Was a Little Lad")

Narrator

We've seen poor Mrs Donoghue, ingested snail inside her
And now we have a precedent with scope that might be wider
The maker of the ginger beer showed total lack of caring
But p'raps this rule of negligence itself needs care bewaring
The notion of a lack of care gave damages for sickness
But might it also compensate for loss of mental fitness?

Example one[1] tells all about some horses in a circus
It needs that we should think about a legal precept's purpose
No duties owed to everyone by persons acting carelessly
Some limitation must prevent too wide responsibility
The rule for mental harm alone? No tortious liability
The harm should be accompanied by patent, actual injury[2]

The plaintiff had a ringside view, a dancing horse before her
When suddenly the horse was caused to back its rump toward her
Disaster struck, upon her lap there fell, with aim unerring
A substance, odoriferous, much laughter this incurring
The point of law – did action lie for mental consternation?
The answer? – yes, was harming her by inj'ry to her person

Example two[3] concerns a plea where courts get in a quandary
For here the victims bring their claims for mental harm that's secondary

....

1   *Christy Bros Circus v Turnage* 144 SE 680 (1928).
2   This was the rule in Georgia, where the case was decided.
3   *Homer v Long* 599 A 2d 1193 (1992)

73

In case of shock-producing acts, some claims the courts won't contemplate
Those where the plaintiff's not involved, in time and space not proximate
He must be there to see and hear a sudden, shocking circumstance
Let's take this rule, apply it to a husband's bad experience

His wife when under strain and stress sought succour from psychiatry
Was counselled on the doctor's couch with extra-special therapy
The husband sued the shrink for shock, the cause his wife's seduction
The treatment going well beyond his wife's mind's deconstruction
The husband's action sadly failed – no claim for such calamity
He was not present at the time. No adequate proximity

Let's turn our minds to number three[4] and give it our attention
This story's slightly stressful so read on with apprehension
The plaintiff's ailing poochie needed vet'rin'ry inspection
So took him off to hospital, in hope of resurrection
"Poor Fido's not so well" she said, "he's clearly rather unfit"
The hospital gave gloomy news – "He's not unwell, he's snuffed it"

---

4   *Corso v Crawford Dog and Cat Hospital* 415 NYS 2d 182 (1979).

A doggie funeral was planned, with last respects and mourning
A casket from the hospital with elaborate adorning
But when the box was opened up, found something else to cry at
Was no dead dog, but there instead the body of a dead cat
The hospital to blame, 'twas held, and liable in tort – a
Grave wrong for making distraught P most certainly distraughter

Some further claims of turpitude show claimants' aspirations
An unplanned child the doctors' due on failing sterilisations?[5]
A losing gambler suing for inadequate prevention?[6]
A victim stuck inside a loo complaining of detention?[7]
What fault might next be said to be an actionable infraction?
The choice will come from everywhere, from all of human action

---

5   *McFarlane v Tayside Health Board* [2000] 2 AC 59. Limited damages.
6   *Calvert v William Hill Credit Ltd* [2009] 2 WLR 1065. No damages.
7   *Sayers v Harlow UDC* [1958] 1 WLR 623. Reduced damages.

A Life of Woe

(Based on *Zepeda v Zepeda* 190 NE 2d 849 (1963))
(Music: THE PIRATES OF PENZANCE: "Oh Is There Not One Maiden Breast")

Plaintiff

I sue here now my wicked sire
His conduct base and all-deceiving
To wed was not his true desire
My mother only too believing
He sought instead to run and roam
All consequences disregarding
A life of woe, no family home
My destiny thus sore retarding
My destiny retarding
A life of woe, no family home
My destiny thus sore retarding

Oh is there not one worthy judge
Accepting truly my privation?
Who willingly will ne'er begrudge
Some kind and ample compensation?
Who'll vindicate and justify
All societal ambition?
And rescue such a one as I
From his adulterine position?
Adulterine position
And rescue such a one as I
From his adulterine position?

Dempsey PJ

This plaintiff blames his origins
Complains about his lowly living
Condemns his father's wicked sins

He's baseborn and he's unforgiving
He grieves his misbegotten birth
No father's name or appellation
And sues for his diminished worth
But fails – no right to vindication
No right to vindication
No claim for his diminished worth
No legal right to vindication

The claimant here could never be
Now telling what he's not obtaining
Without his father wrongfully
Conceiving him – plus his complaining
No harm or hurt or loss incurred
And this must surely bar him claiming
The benefit of life conferred
Can never be a cause for blaming
The benefit of life
The benefit of life conferred
Can never be in law a cause for blaming

Those Supersized Big Macs

(Based on *Pelman v McDonald's Corp* 237 F Supp 2d 512 (SDNY 2003))
(Music: THE GONDOLIERS: "Rising Early in the Morning")

Plaintiffs

Rising early in the morning
When we contemplate our work
And we think of all forewarning
Of those jobs we cannot shirk
We embark without delay
On the duties of the day

First we polish off some batches
Of those supersized Big Macses
And start tucking into fish filet
Then we add some fries and pickles
And tomato sauce that trickles
Down our chins in quite a colourful way
Then we follow up with crispy bacon wraps
Helping fill up all those little extra gaps
Add a Grand or Mighty Angus one or two
Half a dozen quarter pounder burgers too
After that we generally
Take some time to check our tally
And decide we've hardly started – there's a lot of work to do
So we try a few more courses
Each with creamy dipping sauces
'Fore we're pausing and reflecting on some challenges anew
Now in view of cravings inner
We next order up some dinner
Where we finish off more burgers plus some hot fudge apple pie
Then we let our stomachs settle

But we're put upon our mettle
In our planning for our eating that is coming by and by

Oh, our stomachs both are bulging
But we cannot help indulging
For our menu's to our liking and we're satisfied with that
Now we find ourselves competing
About how much we are eating
And it's possible we're getting just a little bit too fat

Chorus

Oh, their stomachs both are bulging
But they cannot help indulging
For their menu's to their liking and they're satisfied with that
Now they find themselves competing
About how much they are eating
And it's possible they're getting just a little bit too fat

Plaintiffs' attorney

In this claim for compensation
From McDonald's Corporation
These poor plaintiffs say their diet made them ill
For their meals were not nutritious
And they're specially suspicious

Of that nasty extra bad cholesterol

'Deed their girths have seen a double-quick increase

So they risk becoming just a bit obese

With McNuggets wholly cooked in oily batter

There's a danger they'll be getting rather fatter

Though they started every morning

Still they did not get a warning

'Bout consuming all those burgers and that other fast food ware

And McDs had placed no label

Listing contents they were able

So the perils from their nurture they could not with ease beware

More, those products were deceiving

So the plaintiffs were believing

They could feed till night and then next day again they could begin

Therefore now we're fully claiming

'Gainst McDonald's, who we're blaming

For these consequences tearful of their wickedness and sin

Oh, defendants who're inclined

To some bad behaviour find

A reluctance to accept their due responsibility

Yet these plaintiffs are unhealthy

While McDs are 'stremely wealthy

And they ought to have to pay for their due liability

Chorus

Oh, defendants who're inclined

To some bad behaviour find

A reluctance to accept their due responsibility

Yet these plaintiffs are unhealthy

While McDs are 'stremely wealthy
And they ought to have to pay for their due liability

Judge Sweet

These two plaintiffs bring proceedings
Which complain about their feedings
On those nuggets, fries and Mighty Macs
With their expectations waning
And no confidence remaining
When they're contemplating all their daily snacks
Say the company's been guilty of deceit
And their cause of action clearly is complete
Very negligent and careless it was too
So damages now payable and due
Yet they ordered more French frieses
Which were all of extra sizes
When were knowing what might happen as resulting from their feed
Then they tried that "Big N' Tasty"
And were rather over-hasty
In consuming every morsel with celerity and speed
For their food afforded pleasure
But they did not like to measure
All their helpings with much needed and severe economy
So they found their weight was gaining
Yet they took no steps constraining
Their inordinate desiring for more fine gastronomy

Oh, those feeling disinclined
To condemn themselves do find
Some reluctance to accept their own responsibility
And of this they're quite forgetful
So this court's not too regretful
In deciding in this case there is no liability

Chorus

Oh, those feeling disinclined

To condemn themselves do find

Some reluctance to accept their own responsibility

And of this they're quite forgetful

So this court's not too regretful

In deciding in this case there is no liability[1]

---

1   The plaintiffs appealed from Judge Sweet's dismissal of their case, and in *Pelman v McDonald's Corp* 396 F 3d 508 (2005) the Appeals Court ruled that the judge had incorrectly dismissed part of the action and that a claim for deceptive advertising could continue. More recently, in *Pelman v McDonald's Corp* No 02-7821, SDNY, 27 October 2010, the District Court held that the claims could not be pursued as a class action, that the plaintiffs had to prove specifically that it was McDonald's food that had caused the plaintiffs' health problems, and that the plaintiffs had to prove that they ate at McDonald's because they believed the food was healthier than it was in fact.

Defamat'ry, Defamat'ry

(Based on *Burton v Crowell Publishing Co* 82 F 2d 154 (1936) and *Berkoff v Burchill*
[1996] 4 All ER 1008)
(Music: THE PIRATES OF PENZANCE: "When You had Left our Pirate Fold")

Lawyer

The judges ponder frequently
On words of rather hurtful sort
Alleged to be defamat'ry
Where action lies in tort
Just how, they ask, can we work out
A test that tells us, certainly
What defamation's all about
And what's defamat'ry?

Chorus

Defamat'ry, defamat'ry
Just what – precisely – can this be?
What insult, smear or slur should be
Most surely held defamat'ry?
What claim against defendant (D)
And brought by angry plaintiff (P)
Complaining, bitterly, can be
Defamat'ry?

Lawyer

Let's check the basis for P's claim
One test – see if the words D spoke
Diminished P's deserved good name
For all right-thinking folk[1]
Test two – what D has said P's done

---

1   *Sim v Stretch* [1936] 2 All ER 1237.

83

Reflects on P most shamefully
So others all most wisely shun
P's nasty company[2]
And now the gist to number three
P's good esteem discredited
With words that were unhappily
In no way merited[3]
Consider now attentively
Test four – a rather different rule –
Exposing P uncaringly
To scorn or ridicule[4]

Chorus

Defamat'ry, defamat'ry
Reflecting shamefully on P
Right-thinkers shun his company
With scorn, disfavour, obloquy
Apply these pointers one, two, three
And four, for surely, as we'll see
The cases tell us what can be
Defamat'ry

Lawyer

Take now a photo, crystal clear
Which shows a scene misleadingly
Where things are not what they appear
Upsetting, sadly, P
Some cigarettes of famous brand
Would "give a lift", you'd "get restored"
Which advert P, with fag in hand
Unhappily deplored

---

2   *Youssoupoff v Metro-Goldwyn-Mayer* (1934) 50 TLR 581.
3   *Scott v Sampson* (1882) 8 QBD 491.
4   *Parmiter v Coupland* (1840) 151 ER 340.

The photo seemed to show the P
With strange appendage juxtaposed
A lewd, grotesque, enormity
Indecently exposed
A visual trick, a clear mirage
Was optic'ly illusory
No denigrating sting or charge
But still defamat'ry[5]

Chorus

Defamat'ry, defamat'ry
A strange appendage we could see
No acting reprehensibly
For optic'ly illusory
It caused for sure ignominy
Although not denigratingly
But still it was, in eyes of P
Defamat'ry

Lawyer

A film review our second case
And true a film director's skin
His shield, his shell, his carapace

---

5   *Burton v Crowell Publishing* Co 82 F 2d 154 (1936).

Must not be extra thin
But D called P a creature foul
With ugly, sour and frightful mien
His features coarse, with sullen scowl
Quite hideous, obscene
This D, a journalist, malign
Here went, it seems, a tad too far
Compared P's face to Frankenstein
Repulsively bizarre

All this was not just comment fair
In principle, accordingly
The words much more than mere hot air
Could be defamat'ry[6]

Chorus

Defamat'ry, defamat'ry
Harsh words describing ugly P
D writing vitriolically
Calls P a gross monstrosity
And thus when others thought of P
They might react repulsively

6   *Berkoff v Burchill* [1996] 4 All ER 1008.

This face to stop a clock could be
Defamat'ry

Lawyer

Insulting words I do submit
Amount to, mostly, uncouth stuff
And so "conniving little shit"
Held not to be enough[7]
But "creep, bombastic fat buffoon"
The P's fair name this did impugn
Was more than just a rude lampoon
The D thus not immune[8]
A theatre critic now, aghast
Thought P's performances so grim
That lavat'ries would jam up fast
(So not impressing him)[9]
And what about "this quivering
And luminously giggling
This mincing, perfumed, sniggering
And fruity-flavoured thing"?[10]

Lawyer and Chorus

Defamat'ry, defamat'ry
Rude words insulting every P
Each claiming, therefore, QED
That D must pay most certainly
For while a disrespectful D
May write of P quite critic'ly
He runs the risk his words will be
Defamat'ry

---

7   *Allason v BBC Worldwide* The Times, 22 January 1998.
8   *Radio 2UE Sydney Pty Ltd v Chesterton* [2009] HCA 16.
9   *Cornwell v Myskow* [1987] 1 WLR 630. A jury found the words to be defamatory, but on appeal a new trial was ordered.
10   *Liberace v Daily Mirror* The Times, 18 June 1959. The words were held to be defamatory.

Porn Shocker

(Based on *Charleston v News Group Newspapers Ltd* [1995] 2 WLR 450)
(Music: IOLANTHE: When You're Lying Awake)

Narrator

Loyal readers unfurled their News of the World
With feelings of nervous anxiety
In the hope of some rude titillation and lewd
Photographs showing gross impropriety
Their hopes were fulfilled and the pages were filled
With much lustful corruption and lechery
With horror and shock, they tried hard to unlock
Their wide eyes from these scenes of debauchery
But quite sadly to say, this salacious display
Showed us stars from TV turned perverted
So the readers, alack, had their eyes drawn right back
To those scenes where they had been averted
The paper amazed and most surely outraged
By this shameless, disgusting porn shocker
From a long-running soap (of Australian scope)
'Bout the life and the times of the ocker

Now the Bishops, from Oz, were famous because
They starred in a series called "Neighbours"
(Soap opera supreme, with an everyday theme
Yet in words of the Bard, somewhat tedious[1])
This respectable pair, with ordinary air
Unassumingly named Madge and Harold
Appeared overheated (though some bits deleted)
Their bodies all closely entangled
"Just what's happ'ning here?" asked the rag "it's so queer
That the Bishops are trying out buggery"

---

1   Much Ado About Nothing, Act III, Scene v, per Leonato: "Neighbours, you are tedious".

Yet 'twas not what it seemed, the article screamed
For the photos were products of fakery
A computerised game should take all the blame
No genuine vice or carnality
It was all just a con, their heads added on
To bodies in films of pornography
"This game we deplore, we're shocked to the core"
Raged the paper in tones quite indignant
"To superimpose a sexual pose
Shows intention that's really malignant
The actors are blameless, the makers are shameless
In profiting from their depravity
It's very upsetting the way that they're getting
At innocent Harold and Madgie"

Yet this kindly address clearly failed to impress
Madge and Harold, who felt discontented
Dragged along through the dirt, their emotions were hurt
Their behaviour still misrepresented
Warm words notwithstanding, the article handing
Them ground for some displeased complaining
The dissembling pathetic and not sympathetic
The friendliness bogus and feigning
So they didn't sit back but went straight on attack
Giving vent to their keen irritation
Consulted the law 'bout a remedy for
An outrageous and base defamation
"It's libel" they said "to suggest that we played
Any part in this sink of concupiscence
Our names are defamed, though another was blamed
And the paper must pay for its insolence"
Their complaint came before those just men of the law
Five stern Lords of Appeal (all in ordinary)
And their Lordships agreed that the case did indeed

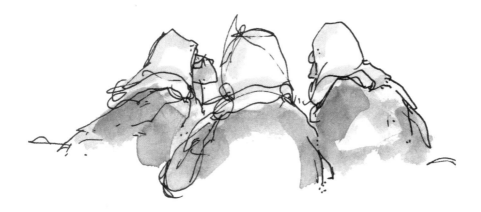

Present facts that were strange and extraordinary
For at least prima facie the photos were racy
With impression quite false and demeaning
Yet the point to decide – Could the newspaper hide
Behind words giving innocent meaning?
Now all would not read nor would take any heed
Of the paper's japanned explanation
Truly some viewers just would gaze at the lust
Suff'ring shock and intense consternation
Could the Bs pick and choose and rely on the views
Of a part of the News o' World's audience?
Or should there be solely one meaning which wholly
Precluded the idea of severance?
Lord Bridge (he of Harwich) thought they did not disparage
Madge and Harold, e'en though they were mortified
The standard demanded – that's a man who's fair minded –
Meant no evil thoughts could be justified
This virtuous creature's a long standing feature
In solving severe disputation
And here with the bane the antidote came
Achieving its neutralisation

So with no one defamed they couldn't be blamed

The newspaper won, the claims all undone

The Bs out of luck, their action unstuck

Sore shamed and abused, indecently used

A lawyerly take on a libellous fake

An assumption indeed that the "readers" could read!

A sorry defence and a general sense

Of a Sunday rag's cant and hypocrisy

But one further thought about what we've been taught

A claim made today just possibly may

Be a tortious misuse of personality

VERY PRIVATE LIVES

AN OPERA IN THREE ACTS

(Based on *Campbell v MGN Ltd* [2004] 2 AC 457 and
Mosley v News Group Newspapers Ltd [2008] EWHC 1777)

CAST

Narrator

Naomi Campbell

Daily Mirror Photographer

Woman E

News of the World Reporter

Counsel for Mr Mosley

Counsel for the *News of the World*

Mr Justice Eady

Chorus

ACT 1

(A street scene outside the premises of Narcotics Anonymous)

Privacy Getting Safeguarding

(Based on *Campbell v MGN Ltd* [2004] 2 AC 457)
(Music: THE YEOMEN OF THE GUARD: "Oh! A Private Buffoon is a
Light-Hearted Loon")

Narrator

Let us cast our minds back to that two-faced attack

On the stars of the saga down under[1]

An alternative claim with its fate not the same

Raised a thought about which we could wonder

P'raps a right long unknown, to be left all alone

Should be getting our closer regarding

So let us reflect on the courts' lucubration

About privacy getting safeguarding

Chorus

Let's give our attention and turn all our thoughts

To the courts' lucubration on finding new torts

And privacy getting safeguarding

(Enter Naomi Campbell, who wanders around looking glamorous)

Narrator

Our story commences in fine circumstances

I'll tell without further preamble

It's a world of high fashion, of drama and passion

---

1   Charleston v News Group Newspapers Ltd [1995] 2 WLR 450, song 'Porn Shocker' above.

And a lady called Naomi Campbell
Celebrity figure, illustrious pillar
Of garmentry, dress and apparel
A true leader in styles, with our eyes she beguiles
She's the world's most superior model

Chorus

A true leader in styles, of refinement and taste
With our eyes she beguiles where she can't be displaced
The world's most superior model

(Ms C starts taking drugs)

Narrator

Yet Ms Campbell's esteem was perhaps just a dream
Claimed a scoop in the *Mirror* newspaper
All its articles aimed at the lives of the famed
And of dirt it was quite a keen scraper
Now Ms Campbell had claimed that she could not be shamed
As a taker of drugs and narcotics
Said we got what we saw, nothing less and no more
(Seems she well understood semiotics)

Chorus

We just got what we saw, all that glitter and gleam
Nothing less and no more, supermodel supreme
For she well understood semiotics

(Enter Daily Mirror *photographer, surreptitiously photographing Ms C)*

Narrator

The sad *Mirror* declaimed the conception was feigned
This disclosed with much ruth and compunction
For their photos all showed that the image bestowed

Had a false and a flattering function
On the catwalks a queen, her life shiny clean
Seemed with virtue Ms C was synonymous
But she'd told porky-pies (that is Cockney for lies)
She belonged to Narcotics Anonymous

Chorus

So she'd told porky pies, not so much as a blush
And she failed to advise without even a flush
She belonged to Narcotics Anonymous

(Ms C berates the photographer)

Narrator

Now I'm sorry to say that without a delay
Ms C told the rag she'd be suing 'em
Most distinctly put out, she had never a doubt
With the win that she'd get she'd be screwing 'em
But the *Mirror* replied that 'twas clear she had lied
Not a libel or false allegation
They had not a care – but they failed to beware
Of a House of Lords brand new creation

Chorus

They had not a care, they just cocked her a snook

But they failed to beware, just a cursory look

At a House of Lords brand new creation

(Rapid exit of photographer followed by an unhappy Ms C)

Narrator

While she could not deny her unfortunate lie

Yet to publish was still not prudential

Could expose that as such, but they'd said much too much

They'd revealed what was most confidential

So the rag most displeased and Ms C well appeased

With a rule we'll consider quite closely

Let us now look at quite what assistance it might

Afford to a Mr Max Mosley

Chorus

We will now look quite hard at their Lordships' new rule

It's perhaps a trump card in proceedings that you'll

Be seeing are brought by Max Mosley

ACT 2

The Racing Car Supremo and the Tart

(Music: HMS PINAFORE: "Kind Captain I've Important Information")

(A sleazy pub. A man and a woman are conversing confidentially at a table)

Woman E

I have a juicy piece of information
For silver I am willing to impart
About a certain intimate relation
Between the race supremo and the tart

Reporter

Good lady in conundrums you are speaking
Though clear your words are coming from the heart
The information I am keenly seeking
Concerns that race supremo and the tart

Both

The racing car supremo
The racing car supremo
Let's talk about that race supremo and the tart

Woman E

The race supremo's favoured predilection
A nonconformist sort of martial art
His conduct needing resolute correction
From discipline that's practised by the tart

99

Reporter

Good evidence about these odd diversions
I clearly need to get before I start
To criticise these acts and cast aspersions
About the race supremo and the tart

Both

The racing car supremo
The racing car supremo
Need proof about the race supremo and the tart

Woman E

I will need to make a clandestine recording
Including every antic à la carte
The information it will be affording
Will put on show the race supremo's tart

Reporter

We'll pay you honest money in the morning
You simply must agree to play your part
Be careful you don't give away a warning
Recording the supremo with the tart

Both

The racing car supremo
The racing car supremo
We're catching out the race supremo with the tart

(Both dance around the table)

Both

Let's celebrate our honourable arrangement
And drink to our success before we part
No danger of a subsequent estrangement
When telling 'bout the race supremo's tart

The racing car supremo
The racing car supremo
We're telling all about the race supremo's tart

(Blackout)

ACT 3

In Flagrante

(Music: TRIAL BY JURY: "Oh Gentlemen Listen I Pray")

(Courtroom scene)

Counsel for Mr Mosley

Your Lordship, please listen I pray
To just why we are taking exception
The newspaper promised to pay
For a plan of deceit and deception
Informed by a lady that she'd
Be happy 'bout upping the ante
For money they slyly agreed
That they'd capture poor M in flagrante
But the papers can't pry and can't nose
In matters of not their concerning
If private concerns they disclose
Have plenty of money for burning

Chorus

But the papers can't pry and can't nose
In matters of not their concerning
If private concerns they disclose
Have plenty of money for burning

Counsel for Mr Mosley

M promised the lady a fee
For applying some corporal correction
All this not intended to be

Something later for public inspection
But the lady concerned – woman E –
For money was over-ambitious
Dispensing some strict third degree
And filming in ways surreptitious
So E and the rag did collude
Such action requires condemnation
It's proper that now we conclude
That they pay for condign compensation

Chorus

So E and the rag did collude
Such action requires condemnation
It's proper that now we conclude
That they pay for condign compensation

Counsel for the *News of the World*

Your Lordship please note what I say
'Bout a story of vice and perversion
It's fitting and meet M should pay
In attracting right-thinkers' aversion
We see this in terms black and white
It's our claim to unbounded expression
For a newspaper's core human right
Is in telling of sexual transgression
This unhappy plaintiff can't sue
And needs to desist from complaining
For what has been said is quite true
There's no right of action remaining

Chorus

This unhappy plaintiff can't sue
And needs to desist from complaining
For what has been said is quite true

There's no right of action remaining

Counsel for the *News of the World*

The public deserved to be told
All about this lubricious activity
Was published for all to behold
A saga of sexual lascivity
For those in a prominent role
Whose conduct demands full exposure
Should pay without fail a full toll
With community good in disclosure
A newspaper's duty is clear
In case of licentious behaviour
Must publish without any fear
Denounce it without any favour

Chorus

A newspaper's duty is clear
In case of licentious behaviour
Must publish without any fear
Denounce it without any favour

They Can't Think Why

(Music: PRINCESS IDA: "If You Give Me Your Attention")

Mr Justice Eady

Recall you how the "Sunday Sport" ensnared poor Mr Kaye[1]
No tort, 'twas held, and now the paper pleads the same today
All's true, they say, there is no case, it's not defamat'ry
And there's public interest in what M did with woman E
But sadly their star witness on her way to court got lost
Put writing on the wall – and now they'll have to pay the cost
No public good or benefit, they need a dressing down
There's no defence, there's not a doubt they're losing all hands down
And they can't think why

Chorus

They can't think why

Mr Justice Eady

The paper says a claim for breach of privacy can chill
If beans are spilled you cannot sue the folk who caused the spill
But Ms Campbell brought an action, and although she had deceived
She still won her claim for damages for feelings most aggrieved[2]
So where it's confidential information in the news
It's not enough it's there for lustful readers to amuse
The claimant is entitled to protect his privacy
He wins his case and is I trust as happy as can be
And they now know why

....

1   *Kaye v Robertson* [1991] FSR 62.
2   *Campbell v MGN Ltd* [2004] 2 AC 457, song 'Privacy Getting
     Safeguarding' above.

106

Chorus

They now know why

Justice Eady and Chorus

Let's see now what a claim for breach of privacy can do

Remember these examples when the focus is on you

Those Chinese waxwork dummies in the Prince's little book[3]

And the Douglas wedding photos that the paparazzi took[4]

Plus intimate behaviour 'tween the Duchess and the Duke[5]

While a picture that embarrasses may need a stern rebuke[6]

So the News o' World, the *Mirror* and an errant fourth estate

Had better take more care or risk a most expensive fate[7]

....

3   *HRH Prince of Wales v Associated Newspapers Ltd* [2008] Ch 57.
4   *Douglas v Hello! Ltd* [2008] 1 AC 1.
5   *Duchess of Argyll v Duke of Argyll* [1967] Ch 302.
6   *Jagger v Darling* [2005] EWHC 683.
7   The *News of the World* unwisely failed to heed this advice, and on
     10 July 2011 it ceased publication.

And we all know why
We all know why

FINIS

A Branding Tool

(Based on *R v Brown* [1994] 1 AC 212)
(Music: PRINCESS IDA: "Whene'er I spoke")

Counsel for the prosecution

A branding tool, equipment you'll
Find warm in application
Through smoke and steam you'll yell and scream
And show disapprobation
Six strokes of cane then six again
Applied with forcibility
Hot blobs of wax, enough to tax
A stoic equanimity
Oh should not those who flog and lash
And whip and scourge and beat and slash
Be charged most unrelentingly
With grievous criminality?

Chorus

We should indeed determinedly
Allege grave criminality

Counsel for the defence

But pause, I pray, a point today
That's thoroughly contested
First ascertain if all the pain
Is actually detested
The stings, the jolts, from fifty volts
They're not at all resented
The throb, the hurt, from switch and quirt
The victims all consented
It may seem strange to you and me

That racking causes ecstasy
But those of outré taste or whim
Are free to gamble life or limb

Chorus

So those of outré taste or whim
Are free to gamble life or limb

Lord Templeman

My Lords, a claim to wound and maim
Shows keen imagination
But still, 'tis true, we may pursue
Self-harming recreation
A drink or smoke does not provoke
Grave penal retribution
And piercing ears creates no fears
Of needful prosecution
Our epidermis too, we think
May benefit from pen and ink
As well, no doubt, there's no misprision
By those performing circumcision

Chorus

As well, no doubt, there's no misprision
By those performing circumcision

Lord Templeman

A victim (V) may well agree
To self-humiliation
But Law Lords we, right-thinkingly
Unite in condemnation
Our judgment's sure (and made de jure)
A ruling that's heuristic
The crime is where the whole affair

Is sado-masochistic
So where there's harm or hurt to V
Behaving masochistically
Convict at once most willingly
No mercy for sadistic B[1]

Chorus

If harming masochistic V
Then throw the book at sadist B

---

1   That is, Brown (the first appellant).

Baked Beans on Toast

(Based on *Ferguson v British Gas Trading Ltd* [2010] 1 WLR 785)
(Music: IOLANTHE: "When I Went to the Bar as a Very Young Man")

Ms Ferguson

My fancy for breakfast is baked beans on toast
Say I to myself say I
But I'll have first of all a quick look at the post
Say I to myself say I
What's this letter I see that has plopped on the mat?
It's a bill for the gas – but I've paid for all that
This irks me a lot so I'm kicking the cat
Say I to myself say I

(Later)

There's no ground for the vapours, it's just a mistake
Say I to myself say I
P'raps their billing department's not fully awake
Say I to myself say I
Then a bit later on comes a bill number two
I write to the senders and say nothing's due
But along come some more, straight out of the blue
Say I to myself say I

(A little later)

I pick up the phone but I cannot get through
Say I to myself say I
A recording just tells me I'm joining a queue
Say I to myself say I
It says now and then that I'm moving ahead
Then horrible tunes once more ring in my head
Much more of all this and my brain will be dead
Say I to myself say I

112

(Later still)

They threaten me now with my gas disconnection
Say I to myself say I
I need to pay up or they'll start debt collection
Say I to myself say I
Court action they say is now planned for my case
My rating for credit an utter disgrace
My cash will be swallowed with never a trace
Say I to myself say I

(Marginally later)

I find my poor teeth are now grinding and gnashing
Say I to myself say I
This is all getting vexing and very harassing
Say I to myself say I
The flow never stops and I'm sure there'll be more
I've had quite enough and I'm off to the law
The legal position I'm keen to explore
Say I to myself say I

(Later on)

My lawyer (who's neither a bumpkin nor hick)
Say I to myself say I
Says there might be an Act that could well do the trick
Say I to myself say I
It aims to protect from harassment and threat

It just might apply to demanding a debt
Those menacing words they'll have cause to regret
Say I to myself say I

(A lot later)

At the hearing it's said I'm just making a fuss
Say I to myself say I
Their line is to argue "Don't blame this on us"
Say I to myself say I
The comp'ny's not guilty, they say, they bemoan
The computer got up to this all on its own
That does I think merit a snort (and a groan)
Say I to myself say I

(And later)

I've won and I'm happy, it's hip hip hooray
Say I to myself say I
Those feeble submissions led no-one astray
Say I to myself say I
The judges have given their knuckles a rapping
You might even call it a kicking and slapping
A day to remember, I'm cheering and clapping
Say I to myself say I

A Writer's Lot

(Based on *British Chiropractic Assoc v Singh* [2011] 1 WLR 133
(Music: THE PIRATES OF PENZANCE: "When a Felon's Not Engaged in his
Employment")

Narrator	When a writer gets engaged in chiropractic
Chorus	Chiropractic
Narrator	And he's looking for some evidence of thought
Chorus	'Dence of thought
Narrator	Then without a doubt he must beware a tactic
Chorus	'Ware a tactic
Narrator	With its aspiration putting him in court
Chorus	Him in court
Narrator	If he makes a rather hurtful imputation
Chorus	Imputation
Narrator	When a disquisitional duty's to be done
Chorus	To be done
Narrator	He might get a cheerless writ for defamation
Chorus	Defamation
Narrator	So a writer's lot is not a happy one
Chorus	Ah
All	When a disquisitional duty's to be done, to be done
	Then a writer's lot is not a happy one, happy one

♪

Narrator	When a writer's faced with matters evidential
Chorus	Evidential
Narrator	And concerning why we might be feeling ill

Chorus	Feeling ill
Narrator	He must check a claim to see if its potential
Chorus	Its potential
Narrator	Comes he thinks to rather more than simply nil
Chorus	Simply nil
Narrator	If it's said the explanation is just spinal
Chorus	Is just spinal
Narrator	Then evaluative duty's to be done
Chorus	To be done
Narrator	It's not necessary that this view be final
Chorus	View be final
Narrator	For his lot is quite a scientific one
Chorus	Ah
All	When evaluative duty's to be done, to be done Then his lot is quite a scientific one, tific one

♪

Narrator	When he looked at what the BCA were claiming
Chorus	A were claiming
Narrator	That good vertebral alignment's all you need
Chorus	All you need
Narrator	Here the writer thought they had to start explaining
Chorus	Start explaining
Narrator	Why there's not a jot of reason for their creed
Chorus	For their creed
Narrator	"It's so bogus", said the writer, "really flaky"
Chorus	Really flaky
Narrator	With such criticising needing to be done

116

Chorus	To be done
Narrator	"All this chiropractic treatment's very shaky"
Chorus	Very shaky
Narrator	And his censure was a very bitter one
Chorus	Ah
All	With this criticising needing to be done, to be done Made his censure such a very bitter one, bitter one

♪

Narrator	But the BCA were not at all contented
Chorus	All contented
Narrator	With this calling into question their repute
Chorus	Their repute
Narrator	Thought the way in which their theory was presented
Chorus	Was presented
Narrator	There was not a need to bother to refute
Chorus	To refute
Narrator	'Cause far better bring a defamation action
Chorus	'Ation action
Narrator	When overbearing duty's to be done
Chorus	To be done
Narrator	And this was, they thought, a suitable reaction
Chorus	'Ble reaction
Narrator	For a libel writ's a very chilling one
Chorus	Ah
All	When overbearing duty's to be done, to be done Here a libel writ's a very chilling one, chilling one

♪

Narrator	So this wrong the plaintiffs claimed deserved redressing
Chorus	'Served redressing
Narrator	In the Royal Courts of Justice in the Strand
Chorus	In the Strand
Narrator	But the writer said their action was suppressing
Chorus	Was suppressing
Narrator	Sincere comment which 'twas clear should not be banned

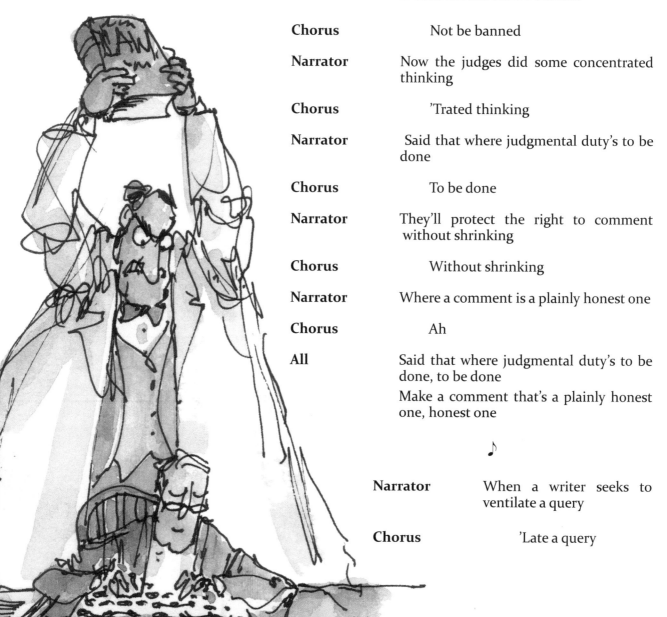

Chorus	Not be banned
Narrator	Now the judges did some concentrated thinking
Chorus	'Trated thinking
Narrator	Said that where judgmental duty's to be done
Chorus	To be done
Narrator	They'll protect the right to comment without shrinking
Chorus	Without shrinking
Narrator	Where a comment is a plainly honest one
Chorus	Ah
All	Said that where judgmental duty's to be done, to be done
	Make a comment that's a plainly honest one, honest one

♪

Narrator	When a writer seeks to ventilate a query
Chorus	'Late a query

Narrator	When a questioner attempts to play the sleuth
Chorus	Play the sleuth
Narrator	We can now feel satisfied there is no dreary
Chorus	Is no dreary
Narrator	Orwellian kind of Ministry of Truth
Chorus	'Stry of Truth
Narrator	If there's something needing serious inquiring
Chorus	'Ous inquiring
Narrator	When investigative duty's to be done
Chorus	To be done
Narrator	Then the writer's surely pleased to be acquiring
Chorus	Be acquiring
Narrator	A new lot that's now a much more happy one
Chorus	Ah
All	When investigative duty's to be done, to be done
	Now the writer's lot's a much more happy one, happy one

♪

Narrator	There is something here I want to state quite clearly
Chorus	State quite clearly
Narrator	Just before I get most earnestly attacked
Chorus	'Ly attacked
Narrator	It's that everything that's said above is merely
Chorus	'Bove is merely

Narrator   Just a comment and opinion and not fact

Chorus   And not fact

All   So when writing song's a duty to be done, to be done
                 Any message is a commentary one, tary one

1. Our Question for the Day Asks if a Promise is Contractual

mat - ters phar - ma - ceu - ti - cal And Mes - srs Boots the chem - ist with their
beat the rule of pri - vi - ty? But C then wants to claim a share and
judge all claims right - mind - ed - ly Lord Den - ning comes to take a stand and
con - tract's u - ni - la - ter - al But don't for - get that deals are made when

mat - ters phar - ma ceu - ti - cal And Mes - srs Boots the chem - ist with their
beat the rule of pri - vi - ty? But C then wants to calaim a share and
judge all claims right - mind - ed - ly Lord Den - ning comes to take a stand and
con - tract's u - ni - la - ter - al But don't for - get that deals are made when

mat - ters phar - ma - ceu - ti - ceu - ti - cal
beat the rule of pri - vi - pri - vi - ty?
judge all claims right mind - ed - mind - ed - ly.
con - tract's u - ni - u - ni - la - ter - al

2.We
3.A
4.So

4

5. And turn-ing now to *Car-lill* and the claim 'bout fumes car-bo-li-cal The

ques-tion's if the smoke-ball pledge is le - gal - ly en-force-a - ble A con-tract with the world at large is

sure - ly in-con-cei - va - ble But don't for - get that deals are made when con-tract's u - ni - la - ter - al.

2. Behold the Smokeball Flu Preventioner

Smokeball Vendor

1.Be - hold the smoke-ball flu pre - ven tion-er   A re - me-dy that's sure - ly ef - fi
2.A re - ward that's found with ev - ery ball   A guar - an-tee that's safe and sat - is

ca - cious No aches or chills or in-flu - en-za nor All o - ther ills or ail-ments or dis-
fact - 'ry One hun-dred pounds we'll glad ly   pay to all Who sniff the ball yet still be-come un

4

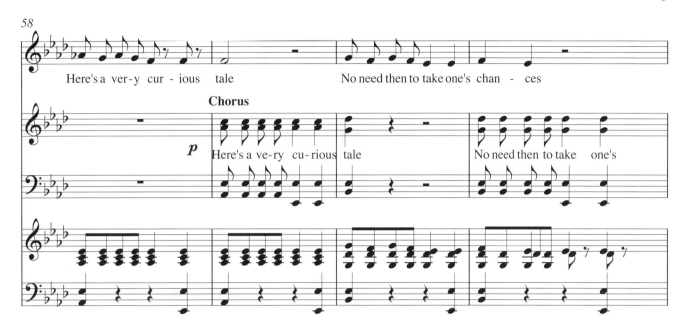

smoke - ball 'flu pre - ven - tion - er!

smoke - ball 'flu pre - ven - tion - er!

smoke - ball 'flu pre - ven - tion - er!

3. Poor Suffering Me

Poor suff-'ring me____ I'm fee-ble, I'm sick-ly, I'm wretch-ed,

Breath'd in the steam, liv-ing a dream, Poor suff-'ring me____ Poor

suff-'ring me____ I'm ail-ing, I'm catch-ing a chill__ Swal-lowed their tales The

re-me-dy fails, I'm poor-ly, I'm suffer-ing, I'm ill. Take heart, don't

2

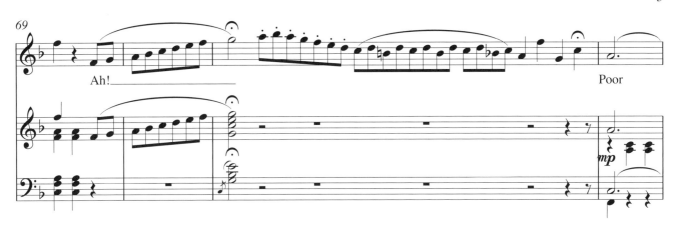

3

Ah!_____ Poor

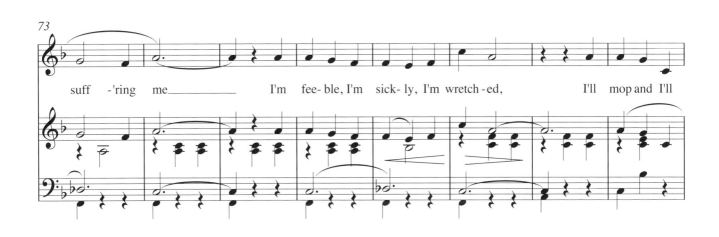

suff -'ring me_____ I'm fee- ble, I'm sick- ly, I'm wretch -ed, I'll mop and I'll

mope but still there is hope of wealth for poor suf -fer - ing me. Ah! ah!

Ah! ah! ah! Ah! ah!_ Ah! ah! ah! Fair days will shine, fair days will

4

(ah)(ah)   (ah) (ah) (ah)_____

_____ ine, Fair   days   will shine!   will   shine!(ah) (ah)_____

ine,   will   shine!

Chorus

Take   heart,   don't wor - ry, don't pine,   sue   for   the

Mrs Carlill

Ah! ah!_____

mo- ney, it's thine.

Ah!_____ it's mine!

4. Silence in Court

Clerk of the Court

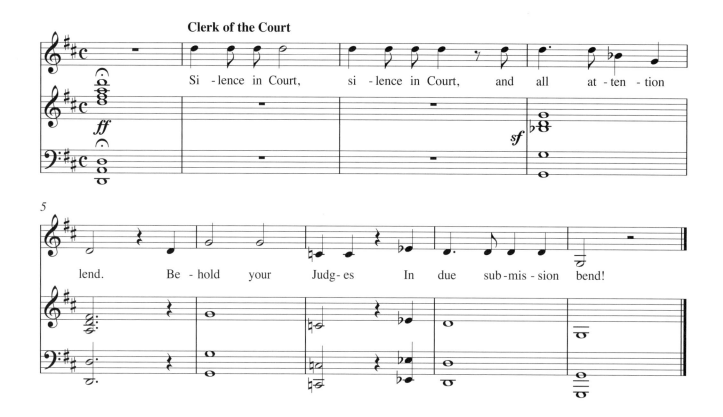

Si - lence in Court, si - lence in Court, and all at - ten - tion lend. Be - hold your Judg- es In due sub - mis - sion bend!

5. My Lords, We Make a Claim Today

Counsel for the Carbolic Smoke Ball Company

from this court she claims her due In_ me-rit-ed com-pen - sa - tion.
judge-ment day has now ar-rived And pay_ we say they ought-er.
aimed her snout right at the trough in the hope of cash ad - van - ces.

4.The post-er's words were but a puff, a bet or gam-ing wa - ger. Con-sid - er -a - tion

not e-nough, 'twas an act of_ God, vis ma - jor. To your Lord- ships learn'd in_ com-mon law we ex-

tend our in - vi - ta -tion: Throw out this suit, this claim of straw with clear_ dis-ap-pro-

rall.

Chorus

ba - tion. To your Lord-ships learn'd in_ com-mon law we ex- tend our in - vi - ta -tion: Throw

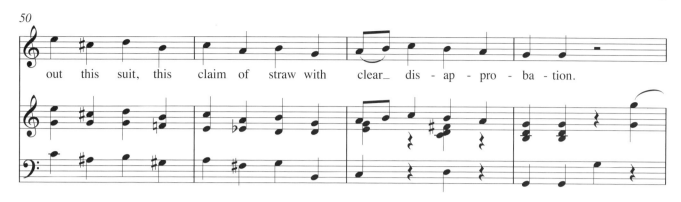

out this suit, this claim of straw with clear_ dis - ap - pro - ba - tion.

6. The Gazette of Pall Mall

Judges 1. The *Gaz - ette* of Pall Mall did an-
Lord Justice Bowen 2. won - drous ball"_ mused
Lord Justice Lindley 3. plain - tiff per- formed her

nounce to us all   'bout a cure that quite won-der-ful - ly   will stop_ the 'flu if you
Mrs - Car-lill,   from flu_ she'd al -ways be free.   She'd ne - ver, she thought, be
side of the pact,   not_ tell-ing de-fen - dant 'D'   Yet tak-ing D's word_ and

buy_ the ball   and sniff it as-sid -uous -ly_____   The com-pa-ny said the
poor - ly or ill,   So grabbed one im-me-diate - ly._____   Her head soon en-wreathed, she
do -ing an act   is per - fect-ly good for me._   When ca -la - mi -ty came and

mon-ey-was paid   with a trus-ty de-po_ sit-ee   A re - ward to all those_ who
gid - di -ly breathed   as_ un -der a sheet_ dove she.   She_ sniff -led and snuff -led and
sick she be -came,   to the comp-'ny she en-tered a plea,   say-ing "Now that I've done it, please

143

6

7. Pepsi Points

1.Now
2.Our
3.An

let's_ sa - lute stout Mrs_ Car - lill No_ doubt_ the read-er re - calls_ She
sto -ry be -gins_ with Pep - si -co___ An -xious'bout mak-ing a pro- fit.
ad on T V_ one sum-mer -y day, in_ terms_ not ve -ry So- crat- ic,

sad - ly caught_ a cold_ and chill,_ af - ter sniff-ing those balls._ She
Keen to mar-ket their drink and so_ peop-le buy lots and lots of it. On
Told all a -bout_ this scheme in a way that might be called mel - o -dram -a -tic

4.

Narrator
Hurricane winds now enter the tale
With booms and crashes and thunder
A teacher is stripped by the storm and the gale
Leaving his wear that was under
Then all is revealed and we see the new prize
And what we are going to get
For landing in front of our goggling eyes
A Harrier AV 8 jet
V 8 jet, V 8 jet, V 8 jet
Chorus
Jumping jet
Narrator
V 8 jet, V 8 jet, V 8 jet
Chorus
Jumping jet
Narrator and Chorus
For landing in front of our goggling eyes
A Harrier AV 8 jet

6.

Narrator
"I wonder just how many points that I've got"
Mused our hero, his hopes very high
On checking it seemed that it wasn't a lot
Fifteen! he found with a sigh
That left him with too much to drink, and hence
He turned to the rules where he saw
That a point could be bought at a cost of ten cents
So he bought seven million more
Seven mill, seven mill, seven mill
Chorus
Million more
Narrator
Seven mill, seven mill, seven mill
Chorus
Million more
Narrator and Chorus
A point could be bought at a cost of ten cents
So he bought seven million more

5.

Narrator
Our plaintiff, John Leonard, had jets on the brain
As a tot at the table he'd thump
And shout "I want a military plane
Especially one that will jump"
Now pondering closely from what he had seen
And how many points he would need
The answer he found at the base of the screen
Seven million points was decreed
Seven mill, seven mill, seven mill
Chorus
Million points
Narrator
Seven mill, seven mill, seven mill
Chorus
Million points
Narrator and Chorus
The answer he found at the base of the screen
Seven million points there decreed

7.

Narrator
Fired off a letter to Pepsico
Claiming his Harrier jet
A cheque for the points as the quid pro quo
All the conditions now met
Awaiting, impatient, his promised reward
He found with increasing chagrin
He waited in vain, his letter ignored
For sadly no jump-jet dropped in
All in vain, all in vain, all in vain
Chorus
Nothing came
Narrator
All in vain, all in vain, all in vain
Chorus
Nothing came
Narrator and Chorus
He waited in vain, his letter ignored
Sadly no jump-jet dropped in

8

Narrator
Our unhappy claimant, with forceful appeal
Went straight way to the court
"It's fraud" he said "They're in breach of the deal
I want the jet that I bought
The commercial misled, the advert deceived
Their practice in trade was unfair
I've reason sufficient to feel a bit peeved
Not getting my military ware"
Feeling peeved, feeling peeved, feeling peeved
Chorus
So deceived
Narrator
Feeling peeved, feeling peeved, feeling peeved
Chorus
So deceived
Narrator and Chorus
Had reason sufficient to feel a bit peeved
Not getting that military ware

9.

Narrator
The rest of this tale I'll sadly relate
A most disappointing report
The claim quickly met an unfortunate fate
Summarily thrown out of court
"'Twas a vision, a simply fantastic joke
In mind of all reasonable folk"
Said the judge, undoubtedly unimpressed
"Nothing more than a joke"
Just a joke, just a joke, just a joke
Chorus
Case dismissed
Narrator
Just a joke, just a joke, just a joke
Chorus
Case dismissed
Narrator and Chorus
The judge undoubtedly unimpressed
Nothing more than a joke

10.

Narrator
So good Mrs C most famously won
Unlucky John Leonard did not
The ad was in fun, JL was undone
This severed the Gordian knot
He was not, it seems, a reasonable man-
That person with far too much unction –
Yet amused us a lot with his pleasing plan
A very commendable function
Pleasing plan, pleasing plan, pleasing plan
Chorus
'Mused us all
Narrator
Pleasing plan, pleasing plan, pleasing plan
Chorus
'Mused us all
Narrator and Chorus
Amused us a lot with his pleasing plan
Very commendable function

8. An Artful Scheme

Narrator

1. LGood Mis - ter Hicks de - vised a com - pe-
2. Miss Chap -lin quick - ly sent an ap - pli
3. De - fen - dant, Mis - ter Hicks had fur - ther

ti - tion, re - veal-ing to us all an art-ful scheme. For la - dies fair, with
ca - tion and read-ers soon were a- ble to be - gin on ex - er - cis - ing
choos - ing, se - lect-ing from the win-ners of each heat. But failed this task, his

fame their clear am- bit - ion, aimed at all those who wished to live their dream. Their
keen dis - cri - mi - na -tion, and spe-ci - fy -ing who they thought should win. All
du - ty thus ab - us - ing. So Miss C then un -ab - le to com - pete Claimed

pho - to - graphs would de-mon-strate their beau-ty. Then read - ers of a pa - per had to choose. Ful-
pho - to - graphs re - quir- ing close pe - rus - ing 'fore mark - ing who de - served to get their tick. No
dam - a - ges on ground of his con - tract-ing to give her an oc - cas - ion for suc - cess, with

9. The Baronet and the Garage Man

ris - to - cra - tic do - nor The Lord of Swy'm - ly Ma - nor and ec - cen-tric a - li - en - or.

Ne - ver mind a per - son's sta-tion Ho-nest pleb or up-per crust Eat the cake with ce - le-bra-tion Class-less be we

sure-ly must.   sure - ly must.

4

10. Is God a Person?

Judge Lander

1. De - fen - dant (D), un - hap - pi - ly is charged with cri - mi - na - li - ty. The crime it's said he did com - mit?(Which D does not at all - ad - mit) 'Twas start - ing lots of for - est fires, such con - duct clear - ly ul - tra vires. Locked up in gaol, and there un - known a ca - me - ra and a

2. "Oh Lord" he prayed "Please give a hand and let me know your least com - mand. I'll do my pen - ance, say my prayers, at - tend my spi - ri - tual - af - fairs. But in re - turn please help a bit, just let me get a - way with it. Please in - ter - vene this once for me. I'll give - my thanks e -

161

3. Judge Lander

Confessed his guilt the police now say
But here some law gets in the way
A record made 'lectronic'ly
Needs speaker's sure authority
Or taping's not permissible
The record inadmissible
"But no" says counsel "incorrect
That argument you must reject
The rule most clearly can't apply
To words directed up on high"

Chorus

The rule most clearly can't apply
To words directed up on high.

4. Judge Lander

Now counsel says there needs to be
Communication, definitely
Words must be spoken you to me
By person A to person B
And here, he says, that's not the case
For no such colloquy took place
 But can this other person be
Almighty God, the Deity?
The question's rather tricky for
A court applying earthly law.

Chorus

The question's rather tricky for
A court applying earthly law.

5. Judge Lander

My mind's made up, I won't convict
The purpose of the law's quite strict
 It aims to safeguard talk and chat
That's private - nothing more than that
Here D intended on his own
To speak with God and God alone
At least in law, and legally
God's got some personality
God is a person, not a doubt
Although He's everywhere about.

Chorus

God is a person, not a doubt
Although He's everywhere about.

11. We Love the Judges' Law

2

165

12. Let's Go to Wellmeadow Cafe

Minchella

sert or a bun or a tart,__ and watch the world pas-sing us by. Good lad-ies, kind greet-ing, de-

light in your eat-ing at Pais-ley's most fab-led ca - fé. These past-ries we're mak-ing, the

cakes that we're bak-ing, please choose from our fin-est ar - ray. We've short-bread and tof-fee, we've

Friend

tea and we've cof-fee, ice-cream and some gin-ger-y beer That sounds just de - li-cious, please

4

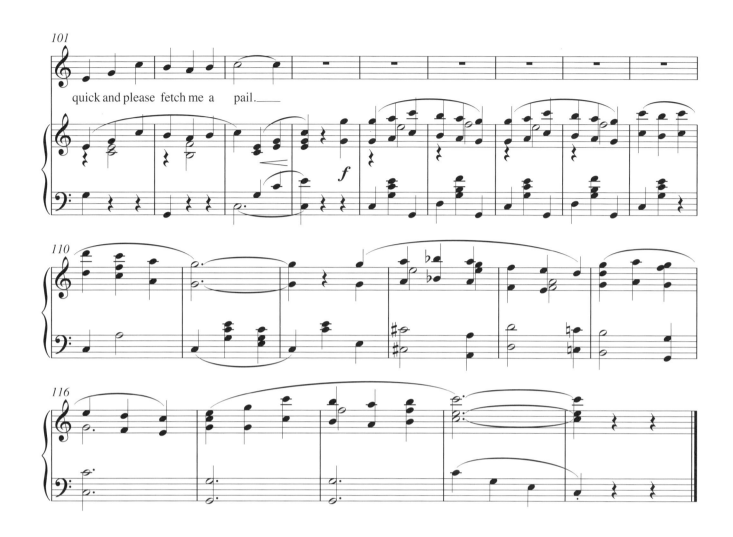

quick and please fetch me a pail.___

13. Entrance of the Peers

Lord Atkin	Esteemed counsel, good morning
Counsel	Sir, good morning
Lord Atkin	I hope you're all quite well
Counsel	Quite well: and you sir?
Lord Atkin	I am in reasonable health, and happy To meet you all once more
Counsel	You do us proud sir.

14. We Are the Judges of the Court of Law

15. Lord Atkin

Andante espressivo

Mrs Donoghue
1. One day   in the sum-mer a
2. I   clutch'd at my bel-ly and
3. The   claim-ant she's fak-ing, no

mar-vel lous treat: **Chorus** Lord At-kin, Lord At-kin, Lord At-kin.   **Mrs.D** In Well-mead-ow Ca - fé, my
fell to the floor: I   sicked, and I sicked, and I
snail in the beer: The fizz   in her glass was trans-

friend there to   meet: **Chorus** Lord   At-kin, Lord At-kin, Lord At-kin.   **Mrs. D** An or - der was made for the
sicked up some more: I gasped and I screamed and I
par - ent-ly   clear: This court, we sub-mit should re-

best gin-ger ale But ad-ded un-known was a well brewed up snail. I__
sobbed and I sighed, I howled and I yelled and I moaned and I cried, An__
ject what she's said. A__ de-com-posed snail on-ly there in her head. A__

Chorus

swal-lowed it down, but then let out a wail:
o-ver-cooked gast-ro-pod in my in-side: Lord At-kin, Lord At-kin, Lord At-kin.
flea in her ear's what she mer-its in-stead:

Chorus

[Counsel for S] 4.Now ev-en ac-cep-ting her sto-ry is true:
[Counsel for Mrs.D] 5.This act-ion con-cerns an e-met-ic af-fair: Lord
[Counsel for Mrs.D] 6.The plain-tiff we say should most sure-ly suc-ceed,

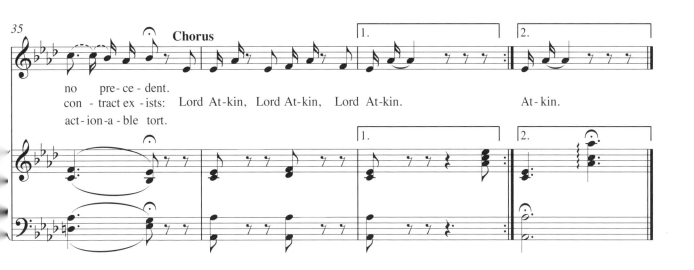

no   pre - ce - dent.
con - tract ex - ists: Lord At-kin, Lord At-kin, Lord At-kin.   At - kin.
act - ion-a - ble tort.

(general hubbub)

(general hubbub)
Clerk of the Court　　Pray silence in court
　　　　　　　　　　　Their Lordships will give their judgement.

16. A Rule of Liabilitee

snails that_ make her ve-ry_ sad - ly ill. There
slugs don't_ make__ his__ drinks im-pure. He
o - d'rous-ly poi - soned Mrs__ Do - no-ghue. He

should we do think most fair- ly be a
must sure-ly act more care-ful -lee and
foots the__ bill and pays the fee and

Chorus

rule___ of___ li -i -a -a -bil -it -ee. There
pay for do -ing wrong to poor-ly Mis-sus D He
com - pen -sates for fail-ing to be neigh-bour-lee. He

should,they do think most fair-ly be a
must sure-ly act more care-ful -lee and
foots the__ bill and pays the fee and

1.2.

rule__ of__ li -i - a -a -bil -i -tee.
pay for do -ing wrong to poor-ly Mis-sus D
com -pen -sates for fail-ing to be

2.We
3.So the

neigh-bour-lee.

17. Trespassing Bees

Moderato

Narrator

p

1.We know the fields of Eng - land green are
2.Here's grow-er (D) with rare con - tent his

loved by those who write po - et - i - cally. But now a plant of a - lien gene in -
rape - seed grow-ing most se - bac-eous ly But shock! Dis - may! With sore tor-ment found

trudes, we think un-sym-pa - the - ti-cally. In art we find from times by - gone the
bugs all chew-ing quite vor - a-cious-ly. Straight-way de - ter - mined, no de - bate and,

tran-quil kine all gra-zing mel-low-ly. But now we find when ga-zing on the fields, we see them shimm-'ring
true to say, with e - qua - ni - mi - ty these bugs he should ex - ter-min-ate (for - get-ting things in close prox-

3. Narrator

Let's turn our thoughts to neighbour (P)
 A man who's working in his apiary
He's studying the honey bee
And keeping bees (a trifle gingerly)
Observe the bees returning home
A multitude that swarms with noisy buzz
 Brings nectar for the honeycomb
For this is what a bee quite often does.
P's disposition now irate
His temperament no more at ease
 No calm, collected mental state
D's conduct certain to displease
 Unhappily, at rapid rate
The grower's spraying killed the bees.
  Chorus
Killed the bees, killed the bees.
 Unhappily, at rapid rate
The grower's spraying killed the bees.

4. Narrator

P's claim in law was swift and strong
"D should have sprayed a lot more cautiously.
The pois'ning was a civil wrong
Behaved without a doubt most tortiously"
"But no", says D, "hear what I say
The scope of tort's not all-encompassing.
Not liable, I need not pay
'Twas very clear the bees were trespassing.
As well, take one of rapeseed's traits
Shows why there was no call for care
A scientific view dictates
The bees need not have been just there.
The rapeseed flower self-pollinates
So blaming me would not be fair."
  Chorus
Not be fair, not be fair
The rapeseed flower self-pollinates
So blaming D would not be fair.

5. Narrator
The judge rejected D's reply
"He's not, D said, at all permitted 'em
Where'er the bees might choose to fly
Would not if asked have then admitted 'em.
Yet sure it was those buzzing bees
The rapeseed flowers would seek out tirelessly.
My view with *Donoghue* agrees
And D's in breach for acting carelessly"
So thoughtless owners all take heed
Self-interest matters not a jot
When spraying plants you must indeed –
Self-pollinating flowers or not –
Take due account of neighbours' need
Else pay what may be quite a lot.
Chorus
Quite a lot, quite a lot
Take due account of neighbours' need
Else pay what may be quite a lot.

18. All of Human Action

23

lack of care gave_	da - ma - ges for sick - ness	But might it al - so com - pen - sate	for
harm a - lone? No__	tor - tious li - a - bi - li - ty	The harm should be ac - com - pan - ied	by
ac - tion lie for__	men - tal con - ster - na - tion?	The an - swer? Yes, was harm - ing her	by

28

D.C

lack of men - tal	fit - ness?
pa - tent, ac - tual	in - ju - ry.
inj' - ry to her	per - son.

4.

Example two concerns a plea where courts get in a quandary
For here the victims bring their claims for mental harm that's secondary
In case of shock-producing acts, some claims the courts won't contemplate
Those where the plaintiff's not involved, in time and space not proximate
He must be there to see and hear a sudden, shocking circumstance
Let's take this rule, apply it to a husband's bad experience

5

A wife when under strain and stress sought succour from psychiatry
Was counselled on the doctor's couch with extra-special therapy
The husband sued the shrink for shock, the cause his wife's seduction
The treatment going well beyond his wife's mind's deconstruction
The husband's action sadly failed - no claim for such calamity
He was not present at the time. No adequate proximity

6

Let's turn our minds to number three and give it our attention
This story's slightly stressful so read on with apprehension
The plaintiff's ailing poochie needed vet'rin'ry inspection
So took him off to hospital, in hope of resurrection
"Poor Fido's not so well" she said, "he's clearly rather unfit"
The hospital gave gloomy news - "he's not unwell, he's snuffed it"

7

A doggie funeral was planned, with last respects and mourning
A casket from the hospital with elaborate adorning
But when the box was opened up, found something else to cry at
Was no dead dog, but there instead the body of a dead cat
The hospital to blame, 'twas held, and liable in tort - a
Grave wrong for making distraught P most certainly distraughter

8

Some further claims of turpitude show claimants' aspirations
An unplanned child the doctors' due on failing sterilisations?
A losing gambler suing for inadequate prevention?
A victim stuck inside a loo complaining of detention?
What fault might next be said to be an actionable infraction?
The choice will come from everywhere, from all of human action

19. A Life of Woe

Slowly

Plaintiff

p
1. I sue here now my wic-ked sire, his
2. Oh is there not one wor-thy judge ac-

con-duct base and all-de-ceiv - ing. To wed was not his true de - sire, my moth-er on - ly too be-
cept-ing tru - ly my pri - va - tion? Who will - ing-ly will ne'er be-grudge some kind and amp-le com-pen

liev-ing. He sought in-stead to run and roam, all con - se-quen-ces dis-re - gar - ding. A
sa - tion? Who'll vin - di -cate and just - i - fy all so - ci - et-al am-bi - tion? And

life of woe, no fam-ily home, my des -ti -ny thus so re re - tard-ing, my des - ti -ny re -
res - cue such a one as I from his a-dul-ter-ine po - sit -ion, a - dul-ter-ine po-

tard-ing. A life of woe, no fam-ily home, my des - ti - ny thus so re re-tar - ding.
sit - ion. And res - cue such a one as I from his_ a - dul-ter - ine po-sit - ion?

2.Oh
3. This plain - tiff blames his
4. claim - ant here could

Dempsey PJ

le - gal_ right to vin - dic-a - tion.
ne - ver be in law a

4. The

cause for bla - ming.

20. Those Supersized Big Macs

4

21. Defamat'ry, Defamat'ry

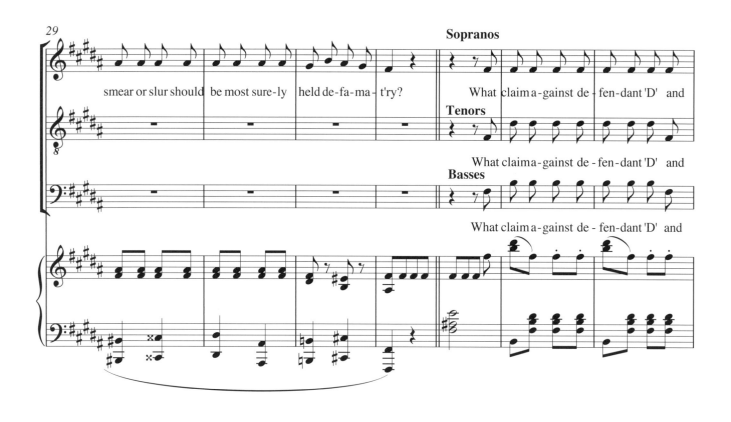

3. Lawyer

Take now a photo, crystal clear
Which shows a scene misleadingly
Where things are not what they appear
Upsetting, sadly, P
Some cigarettes of famous brand
Would "give a lift", you'd "get restored"
Which advert P, with fag in hand
Unhappily deplored
The photo seemed to show the P
With strange appendage juxtaposed
A lewd, grotesque, enormity
Indecently exposed
A visual trick, a clear mirage
Was optic'ly illusory
No denigrating sting or charge
But still defamat'ry

Chorus

Defamat'ry, defamat'ry
A strange appendage we could see
No acting reprehensibly
For optic'ly illusory
It caused for sure ignominy
Although not denigratingly
But still it was, in eyes of P
 Defamat'ry

4. Lawyer

A film review our second case
And true a film director's skin
His shield, his shell, his carapace
Must not be extra thin
But D called P a creature foul
With ugly, sour and frightful mien
His features coarse, with sullen scowl
Quite hideous, obscene
This D, a journalist, malign
Here went, it seems, a tad too far
Compared P's face to Frankenstein
Repulsively bizarre
All this was not just comment fair
In principle, accordingly
The words much more than mere hot air
Could be defamat'ry

Chorus

Defamat'ry, defamat'ry
Harsh words describing ugly P
D writing vitriolically
P's face a gross monstrosity
And thus when others thought of P
They might react repulsively
This face to stop a clock could be
Defamatr'ry

5. Lawyer

Insulting words I do submit
Amount to, mostly, uncouth stuff
And so "conniving little shit"
Held not to be enough
But "creep, bombastic fat buffoon"
The P's fair name this did impugn
Was more than just a rude lampoon
The D thus not immune
A theatre critic now, aghast
Thought P's performances so grim
That lavat'ries would jam up fast
(So not impressing him)
And what about "this quivering
And luminously giggling
This mincing, perfumed, sniggering
And fruity-flavoured thing"?

Lawyer and Chorus

Defamat'ry, defamat'ry
Rude words insulting every P
Each claiming, therefore, QED
That D must pay most certainly
For while a disrespectful D
May write of P quite critic'ly
He runs the risk his words will be
Defamat'ry

22. Porn Shocker

4

5

204

names are de-famed,though an - o - ther was blamed and the pa - per must pay for its in-so-lence. 4.Their com-
should there be sole - ly one mean-ing which whol - ly pre - clu - ded the i - dea of

se - ver - ance. Lord Bridge (he of Har - wich thought they did not dis - pa - rage Madge and

Ha - rold, e'en though they were mor - ti - fied. The stan-dard de-man-ded-that's a man who's fair-min-ded-meant

no e - vil thoughts could be jus-ti - fied. This vir - tu - ous crea-ture's a long stand-ing fea-ture in

po-cri-cy
But one fur - ther thought a - bout what we've been
taught a claim made to-day just pos - sib-ly may Be a tor-tious misuse of per - son - a - li - ty.

23. Privacy Getting Safeguarding

4.
Narrator
The sad Mirror declaimed
The conception was feigned
This disclosed with much ruth and compunction
For their photos all showed
That the image bestowed
Had a false and a flattering function
On the catwalks a queen
Her life shiny clean
Seemed with virtue Ms C was synonymous
But she'd told porky-pies
(That is Cockney for lies)
She belonged to Narcotics Anonymous
Chorus
So she'd told porky pies
Not so much as a blush
And she failed to advise
Without even a flush
She belonged to Narcotics Anonymous

5.
Narrator
Now I'm sorry to say
That without a delay
Ms C told the rag she'd be suing 'em
Most distinctly put out
She had never a doubt
With the win that she'd get she'd be screwing 'em
But the Mirror replied
That 'twas clear she had lied
Not a libel or false allegation
They had not a care -
But they failed to beware
Of a House of Lords brand new creation
Chorus
They had not a care
They just cocked her a snook
But they failed to beware
Just a cursory look
At a House of Lords brand new creation

6.
Narrator
While she could not deny
Her unfortunate lie
Yet to publish was still not prudential
Could expose that as such
But they'd said much too much
They'd revealed what was most confidential
So the rag most displeased
And Ms C well appeased
With a rule we'll consider quite closely
Let us now look at quite
What assistance it might
Afford to a Mr Max Mosley
Chorus
We will now look quite hard
At their Lordships' new rule
It's perhaps a trump card
In proceedings that you'll
Be seeing are brought by Max Mosley

24. The Racing Car Supremo and the Tart

Woman E 3.The
Reporter 5.I will
Both 7.Let's

25. In Flagrante

28

close__ have plen-ty of mo-ney for burn-ing But the pa-pers can't pry and can't nose in
clude that they pay for con-dign com-pen-sa-tion So__ E and the rag did col-lude Such
true__ there's no right of ac-tion re-main-ing This__ un-hap-py plain-tiff can't sue and
fear__ De-nounce it with-out a-ny fa-vour A__ news-pa-per's du-ty is clear In

33

mat-ters of not their con-cern-ing If pri-vate con-cerns they dis-
ac-tion re-quires con-dem-na-tion It's pro-per that now we con-
needs to de-sist from com-plain-ing For what has been said is quite
case of li-cen-tious be-ha-viour Must pub-lish with-out a-ny

36

1.
close__ have plen-ty of mo-ney for burn-ing.
clude that they pay for con-dign com-pen-sa-tion.
true__ there's no right of ac-tion re-main-ing
fear__ de-nounce it with-out a-ny

2.
2.M
3.Your
4.The
fa-vour.

26. They Can't Think Why

2

27. A Branding Tool

Counsel for the Prosecution 1.A brand-ing tool, e - quip-ment you'll find warm in ap - pli - ca - tion Through
Counsel for the Defence 2.But pause, I pray, a point to - day that's tho-rough-ly con - tes - ted First

smoke and steam you'll yell and scream and show dis - ap-prob - a - tion. Six
as - cer - tain if all the pain is ac-tual-ly de - tes - ted The

strokes of cane then six a - gain ap - plied with for-ci - bi-li-ty, Hot blobs of wax, e - nough to tax a
stings, the jolts, from fif - ty volts, they're not at all re - sen - ted The throb, the hurt, from switch and quirt, the

Chorus

4

well,   no doubt, there's   no   mis - pri - sion by   those per - form - ing   cir - cum - ci - sion.
harm   -   ing ma - so - chis - tic   V___   then   throw   the   book   at

sa - dist B.

28. Baked Beans on Toast

5. I find my poor teeth are now grinding and gnashing
Say I to myself, say I
This all getting vexing and very harassing
Say I to myself, say I
The flow never stops and I'm sure there'll be more
I've had quite enough and I'm off to the law
The legal position I'm keen to explore
Say I to myself, say I

6. My lawyer (who's neither a bumpkin nor hick)
Say I to myself, say I
Says there might be an Act that could well do the trick
Says I to myself, say I
It aims to protect from harassment and threat
It might just apply to demanding a debt
Those menacing words they'll have cause to regret
Say I to myself, say I

7. At the hearing it's said I'm just making a fuss
Say I to myself, say I
Their line is to argue "Don't blame this on us"
Say I to myself, say I
The comp'ny's not guilty, they say, they bemoan
The computer got up to this all on its own
That does I think merit a snort and a groan
Says I to myself, say I

8. I've won and I'm happy, it's hip hip hooray
Say I to myself, say I
Those feeble submissions led no-one astray
Say I to myself, say I
The judges have given their knuckles a rapping
You migh even call it a kicking and slapping
A day to remember, I'm cheering and clapping
Say I to myself, say I

29. A Writer's Lot

226

3

4.

Narrator	But the BCA were not at all contented
Chorus	All contented
Narrator	With this calling into question their repute
Chorus	Their repute
Narrator	Thought the way in which their theory was presented
Chorus	Was presented
Narrator	There was not a need to bother to refute
Chorus	To refute
Narrator	'Cause far better bring a defamation action
Chorus	'Ation action
Narrator	When overbearing duty's to be done
Chorus	To be done
Narrator	And this was, they thought, a suitable reaction
Chorus	'Ble reaction
Narrator	For a libel writ's a very chilling one
Chorus	Ah
All	When overbearing duty's to be done, to be done Here a libel writ's a very chilling one, chilling one

5.

Narrator	So this wrong the plaintiffs claimed deserved redressing
Chorus	'Served redressing
Narrator	In the Royal Courts of Justice in the Strand
Chorus	In the Strand
Narrator	But the writer said their action was suppressing
Chorus	Was suppressing
Narrator	Sincere comment which 'twas clear should not be banned
Chorus	Not be banned
Narrator	Now the judges did some concentrated thinking
Chorus	'Trated thinking
Narrator	Said that where judgmental duty's to be done
Chorus	To be done
Narrator	They'll protect the right to comment without shrinking
Chorus	Without shrinking
Narrator	Where a comment is a plainly honest one
Chorus	Ah
All	Said that where judgmental duty's to be done, to be done Make a comment that's a plainly honest one, honest one

6

Narrator	When a writer seeks to ventilate a query
Chorus	'Late a query
Narrator	When a questioner attempts to play the sleuth
Chorus	Play the sleuth
Narrator	We can now feel satisfied there is no dreary
Chorus	Is no dreary
Narrator	Orwellian kind of Ministry of Truth
Chorus	'Stry of Truth
Narrator	If there's something needing serious inquiring
Chorus	'Ous inquiring
Narrator	When investigative duty's to be done
Chorus	To be done
Narrator	Then the writer's surely pleased to be acquiring
Chorus	Be acquiring
Narrator	A new lot that's now a much more happy one
Chorus	Ah
All	When investigative duty's to be done, to be done Now the writer's lot's a much more happy one, happy one